PREPARE YOURSELF
TO BE LUCKY

www.amplifypublishing.com

Prepare Yourself to Be Lucky: Spirited Lessons to Cultivate Business Success

I have tried to recreate events, locales, and conversations from my memories of them. In order to maintain their anonymity in some instances I have changed the names of individuals and places. I may have changed some identifying characteristics and details such as physical properties, occupations, and places of residence.

For more information, please contact:
Amplify Publishing, an imprint of Mascot Books
620 Herndon Parkway #320
Herndon, VA 20170
info@amplifypublishing.com

Library of Congress Control Number: 2021910340

CPSIA Code: PFRE0721A
ISBN-13: 978-1-63755-041-0

Printed in Canada

*I dedicate this book to my grandson, Patrick, and to all the
young adults about to begin college and embark on their
careers. Work hard, listen wisely, take advantage of every
opportunity, and most of all, have fun.*

PREPARE YOURSELF
TO BE
LUCKY

SPIRITED LESSONS
TO CULTIVATE BUSINESS SUCCESS

ED McDONNELL
FORMER PRESIDENT AND CEO
SEAGRAM'S SPIRITS AND WINE GROUP

amplify

Graduated from
Suffolk University

Married Catherine
(Kay) McNamara

1959–1961
Worked at Federated
Department Stores

Born in Boston,
Massachusetts

1935

1959

Son Paul born

1962

1953

1953–1955
Military service,
US Army

1961

Son Edward F.
McDonnell Jr. (Ted) born

1961–1964
Worked at Raytheon

ED McDONNELL TIMELINE

1966–1975
Worked at General Foods

1966

1981–1995
Worked at Seagram

1981

Kay McDonnell's
death

2012

1965

Daughter Elizabeth
(Beth) born

1975

1975–1981
Worked at Pillsbury

1995

1995–2012
Owned and operated
Premier Wine and Spirits

ACKNOWLEDGMENTS

To my son Paul, thank you for helping me put this book together.

I am also thankful to the late Edgar Bronfman Sr., who believed in me from day one and allowed me to hit the ground running in building the Seagram Company into one of the largest international beverage alcohol companies in the world. Together we shared significant successes and an occasional failure, yet we always remained loyal and the best of friends. Thanks for the ride of a lifetime, Edgar!

Many thanks to Hope Lika, whose encouragement and support helped me create the vision for this book.

My appreciation also goes to Alice Lesch Kelly, whose talents as an interviewer, researcher, and writer helped bring my story to life.

Finally, thanks to the many family members, friends, and colleagues who took the time to share their memories, including:

Marty Bart

Bill Bowen

James Espey

Mary Garrard

Stephen Herbits

Ken Herich

Vivienne Hylton

Marisa Kelly

Mollie Kirchner

Fernando Kfouri

Hope Lika

Peggy McDonnell Malley

Beth McDonnell

John McDonnell

Paul McDonnell

Patrick McDonnell

Ted McDonnell

Bill O'Neill

Tony Rodriguez

Jan Roeder

Peter Schreer

Sonia Uzun Tenorio

Alex von Bidder

Andy Teubner

CONTENTS

INTRODUCTION

UNTIL RECENTLY, IT NEVER WOULD HAVE OCCURRED TO ME TO WRITE A BOOK. But then two things happened that made me think it might be a good idea.

The first occurred in the fall of 2019. I attended a wonderful ceremony celebrating the scholarship program I have funded for nearly twenty-five years at Suffolk University, my alma mater. The McDonnell Scholars Program has supported three hundred Suffolk business students participating in intensive international travel seminars in countries around the world.

One of the reasons I funded this program is that I understand, after a long, successful career in global business, how valuable it is for business students to have international experiences early in their careers. Growing up as the son of poor Irish immigrants in South Boston, I never even went to Cape Cod, let alone other countries. But my career took me all over the globe, and seeing the world taught me lessons about business and myself that I never would have learned if I'd stayed home. With the McDonnell Scholars Program, I wanted to give promising Suffolk business students— many of whom are children of immigrants and first-generation college students who have never traveled outside the United States—some exposure to worlds beyond their own. Today, business is global, and if you don't have experience with other cultures, you're at a disadvantage.

Among the attendees at the McDonnell Scholars celebration that day were several students who had taken part in the program. Two of the students, Mayra Gonzalez and Steven Lopez, spoke eloquently about their travel experiences—Israel for Mayra and China for Steven. During their travel seminars, McDonnell Scholars learn about business and cultural practices in their host countries through a variety of experiences, including intensive projects and on-site visits to various companies and organizations. Both Mayra and Steven raved about the experience, and I felt so proud of them and all the McDonnell Scholars. What an honor for me to have the opportunity to contribute to their success.

While we chatted after the ceremony, several of the students asked me for advice about their careers. This happens fairly often; over the years, many McDonnell Scholars and other young people with an interest in business have reached out to me. I always enjoy talking with them, not only because I am happy to answer questions and offer guidance but because I see myself in them. I enjoyed the heck out of my career, and now that I'm retired, I appreciate knowing that some of the lessons I've learned might help others.

College classes teach business basics, of course, but so much of what businesspeople need to know comes from the knowledge and experiences of those who came before them. Old-timers like me owe it to our younger colleagues to share what we've learned. What better way to do that than to write a book? And so, my desire to share my experiences and advice with promising young people like Mayra and Steven—as well as my grandson, Patrick, who is just starting to think about things like jobs and careers—is the first reason I'm embarking on this project.

The second reason entered my mind during a birthday party I attended around the same time as the McDonnell Scholars celebration at Suffolk. My dear friend and longtime colleague Fernando Kfouri is known for his parties, and when he turned eighty, he threw a huge bash. Even though Fernando lives in São Paulo, Brazil, he had his party in Manhattan because it was a central meeting spot for friends around the world. Fernando and I worked together for many years, first at General Foods and then at the Seagram Company, from which I retired in 1995 as president and chief executive officer of the Spirits and Wine Group.

Fernando's party was a reunion of sorts, drawing friends and former colleagues from all over. Many of us had worked together for years, even decades. As I moved from company to company and country to country during the course of my career, I often brought others with me, surrounding myself with talented people I believed in and trusted. During the birthday party, we all had a fabulous time telling tales from our days living and working and traveling abroad in Europe, South America, Asia, and the Caribbean. We had so many stories, so much shared history, and I realized during that party that I wanted to capture those stories and put them down on paper. They were too important to lose with the passing of time.

These memories matter not just because they are important to me and the people I worked with but because they give an up-close view of some of the most influential companies, industries, and business trends of the twentieth century.

In writing this book, I'm setting out to preserve those stories not just for my family, friends, and colleagues but for posterity. (Incidentally, although I wrote this book from my point of view, I've asked others to share their perspectives as well.) While many of the details of these stories are personal, the big picture is actually quite universal. When I started my career in the 1960s, major US companies focused primarily on their domestic business—generally, markets in other countries contributed little or nothing to their bottom lines. But globalism brought about dramatic changes in the 1970s, '80s, '90s, and beyond, and companies like the ones I worked for—Raytheon, General Foods, Pillsbury, Seagram, and then my own company, Premier Wine and Spirits—embarked on tremendous international expansions that transformed the business world and global economies. Talk about being in the right place at the right time: my colleagues and I were lucky enough to be leading major companies during one of the most exciting times in corporate history.

The business world has changed dramatically since I started out, and it has continued to evolve even since I retired a few years ago. Organizations are more diverse, although we still have plenty of work to do in that area. Globalism is a fact of life, even for the smallest companies. And technology plays an increasingly important and ever-changing role in business. But some things haven't changed, like the need for hard work, creativity, and perseverance. In more ways than you might realize, the skills I needed to succeed in my career are remarkably similar to what works today: Step out of your comfort zone. Do the right thing. Think big. Build a good team. Listen more than you talk. Know when to walk away. And most important of all, in my view: prepare yourself to be lucky because you just never know when an opportunity is going to come along.

I don't claim to know everything about business—or life, for that matter—but I do know a few things. I look forward to sharing them in this book and telling some stories along the way, too.

1

PREPARE YOURSELF
TO BE LUCKY

WHEN I LEFT WORK ON A SNOWY EVENING IN 1967, I HAD NO IDEA THAT I WAS ABOUT TO HAVE ONE OF THE MOST IMPORTANT EXPERIENCES OF MY LIFE.

As a financial analyst at General Foods in White Plains, New York, I had the job of keeping an eye on the company's overseas businesses. The international division was just a small part of General Foods at that time, and many of its holdings in other countries didn't perform especially well. Today, we take globalism for granted, but back then, even the biggest US companies focused primarily on their domestic business.

Although I was not on the corporate fast track at General Foods, I had already achieved astonishing success in my career. Astonishing for me, anyway. The child of uneducated Irish immigrants, I had grown up poor in a family that believed in hard work but had no use for higher education. The first time I ever saw my father cry was when I told him I planned to go into the army for two years as a draft volunteer so I could get the GI Bill to pay for a college education. My father could never understand why I would want to break up our family by doing so. Never mind that the college I would attend, Suffolk University, was only about ten miles away and that I'd be living at home while attending school. In my father's mind, going to college just didn't make sense when I could have gotten a perfectly good job in the grocery store down the block.

I had great respect for the blue-collar workers in my family and my neighborhood. I saw how hard they worked to feed their families and pursue the American dream. Perseverance allowed my parents—a farm boy from County Roscommon, Ireland, and a servant girl from County Cork who met at a "Maid's Night Out" social at the Hibernian Hall in Roxbury, Massachusetts—to have three children and end up owning a small six-room brick house in Hyde Park. But my father wore himself out doing jobs like shoveling coal and making sure the electricity worked in commercial buildings. I wanted more than that from life.

When I was in elementary school, my teachers encouraged me to take the exam for Boston Latin, an academically rigorous high school in Boston. Although Boston Latin had educated the children of upper-class Boston Brahmin families for three hundred years, it was a free public school that granted entrance to any seventh grader, rich or poor, who scored above a certain level on its entrance exam. And to this day, it still does. Acing that test and going to Boston Latin not only gave me a better education than I would have received at Hyde Park High but it exposed me to a very different way of life than the one in which I had been raised. When classmates from wealthy families invited me to their houses in Back Bay or Beacon Hill or Brookline, I looked around at their homes and thought: *this* is the life I want.

But I had no money for college, so after high school, I spent two years in the army to have access to the GI Bill. For so many people like me— first-generation Americans raised in poverty—the GI Bill provided a free college education and entry to the middle class. There's no way that I or any of the other kids in my neighborhood could have gone to college without it.

• • •

After college, I landed a job as an auditor for a company in New York City. One job led to another, and in my early thirties, I found myself working as a financial analyst at General Foods. I had already come so far—I had spent a couple of years working in London, first for Raytheon Technologies and then for General Foods. But on this snowy evening, after a long day crunching numbers and preparing reports about General Foods' international subsidiaries, I packed up my briefcase, pulled on my overcoat, stepped into my galoshes, and headed out to my car for a slippery drive home. As I walked out of the building, I noticed another fellow leaving at the same time. He didn't know me, but I certainly knew him: George Bremser Jr., the president of General Foods.

In the parking lot, I scraped the snow off my windshield and turned the heater on high. I wasn't looking forward to the drive to my home in Ridgefield, Connecticut, which took at least forty minutes on an ordinary evening. But I figured I'd pass the time listening to the radio, catching up on the news or humming along to some of the classical music I enjoyed so much.

Just as I was about to drive out of the parking lot, I heard the whining sound of a car that wouldn't start. I looked over and saw that the unlucky driver with the uncooperative car was Mr. Bremser. I got out of my car to see if I could give him a hand.

"Mr. Bremser, I'm Ed McDonnell," I said. "I work for the company. Is there anything I can do for you?"

"Well, you can get my damn car started," he said. But it was no use.

That car wasn't going anywhere without a tow truck, which would take hours to arrive on a snowy evening like this.

"Can I drive you home?" I offered. "I go by the town where you live. I'd be happy to drop you off."

"Sure," Mr. Bremser said. "Thank you very much, son. That would be perfect."

And so we set off.

The snow worsened, and the traffic on the Merritt Parkway came to a stop. We were in for a long trip. But Mr. Bremser was a friendly person, and I always enjoyed talking with new people. We hit it off right away, chatting about this and that. Eventually our conversation came around to work.

"Son, tell me what you do for the company," Mr. Bremser said. I liked my job and was happy to talk about it. I explained how I analyzed the performance of various overseas businesses owned by General Foods. During the course of the long drive—we spent a couple of hours together in the car—I answered all of his questions about our international businesses. Which ones were doing well? Which ones were doing poorly? What drove the success of high-performing businesses and the failures of poor performers? Although Mr. Bremser was the president of the company, he was not that knowledgeable about the specifics of the international business, which tells you something about the priority that General Foods placed on its non-US holdings at that time.

I didn't hold back when answering Mr. Bremser's questions. I was diplomatic, of course, but I was also honest. I had studied our oversees holdings quite closely. It was my job to understand what was going on behind the scenes at these places, including their strengths and weaknesses, and I took that job seriously. I welcomed the opportunity to share my assessments with Mr. Bremser, and he seemed fascinated to hear them.

Shortly before we reached Mr. Bremser's home, he asked me a question that ended up changing my life—although back then, it seemed like just another part of the conversation. In any other setting, such as a meeting, I might not have answered it so frankly. But in the car, on that snowy evening, after sitting in traffic for so long with this genial man, I felt comfortable being completely candid.

"Of all our international holdings," Mr. Bremser asked, "which one is in the worst shape?"

"No question about it," I responded. "Kibon, a food products producer and the largest ice cream company in Brazil, which we acquired a few years ago. It's a mess. It has huge potential, but it's never made a penny."

"Tell me more," he said. So I did.

A few days later, Mr. Bremser called me into his office. This was highly unusual—the president of General Foods doesn't summon a lower-level financial analyst just to chat. I wondered if I had offended him or spoken out of turn in the car. But that couldn't have been it. I felt sure that Mr. Bremser had enjoyed our conversation and was interested in everything I had to say.

I went up to the executive suite, a beautifully decorated set of offices with deep carpeting and luxurious furniture. After I spent a few minutes waiting, his secretary showed me into his office. We shook hands, and he thanked me for giving him a ride.

And then he offered me a new job.

He wanted me to be his assistant.

Wow.

Let me explain what it meant to be chosen to serve as assistant to the president at General Foods. The men chosen for that position—and back in the 1960s, it was a job that went only to men—would work closely with the president for one year and would then be promoted to top management positions throughout the company. Although in my dreams I had imagined moving up the General Foods corporate ladder in this way, I fully understood the unlikeliness of it. Men picked to serve as assistant to the president were Harvard Business School graduates from elite families. They were tall, handsome, and Protestant. They certainly weren't Irish-Catholic kids from South Boston who had put themselves through Suffolk University on the GI Bill.

But Mr. Bremser saw something in me that he liked enough to give me that job. And when it was time to ship me off to another position in the company a year later, he showed that he hadn't forgotten that snowy evening in my car.

"I'm going to send you down to Kibon in Brazil," Mr. Bremser said.

The idea of an international posting thrilled me—I had loved living in London a few years earlier, working first for Raytheon and then for General Foods, before being transferred back to headquarters in White Plains. But I hesitated because of the potential challenges I'd face. "I appreciate your confidence, Mr. Bremser, but Kibon is the most troubled company we own," I said. "Plus, I don't know Portuguese. And I don't know anything about the ins and outs of living in Brazil."

But Mr. Bremser brushed aside my concerns. "With your attitude and your professionalism, you'll figure all that out," he said. "I can't think of a better place for you to get your hands dirty. I want you to go to Brazil and fix Kibon. Turn it around. Make it profitable."

And that's exactly what I did. By the time I left Kibon eight years later, it was one of General Foods' most profitable international companies. And for me, it was the beginning of a fabulous international career that eventually led me to the Seagram Company, where I ultimately served as president and CEO of its $5 billion Spirits and Wine Group.

When I reflect back on this story, I'm astonished to think about how many different strokes of luck had to occur in order for me to end up where I did. What if it hadn't snowed in White Plains that evening? What if Mr. Bremser hadn't had car trouble? What if I had left work five minutes later and somebody else had offered him a ride? My whole life might have been completely different.

Spending those hours in the car with George Bremser was a huge lucky break, but it was a break for which I was prepared. Ever since I was a kid, I had been preparing myself to be lucky. When I took the entrance exam for Boston Latin, I was preparing myself to be lucky. When I used the GI Bill to go to college, I was preparing myself to be lucky. When I worked long hours analyzing the strengths and weaknesses of General Foods' international businesses, I was preparing myself to be lucky. When good luck came my way in the snowstorm that night, I was fully prepared to make the most of it. I'd been working hard at my job at General Foods, and when Mr. Bremser asked me for my opinions and assessment of the company's international business holdings, I took full advantage of that opportunity by giving him the shrewd analysis he wanted. I had no idea when an opportunity to shine might come along, but when it did, I was ready. I had prepared myself to be lucky.

I had figured out pretty early in life that we can't control our luck, but we can set our sights high and work extremely hard so that when luck does come our way, we can make the most of it. Because you just never know when a fantastic opportunity—or a major snowstorm—will come along.

• • •

It's not enough just to prepare yourself to be lucky. You also have to be ready to make the most of any luck that comes along—even if you're not sure whether the luck you're having is good or bad.

Although I didn't realize it at the time, the job I held during college helped prepare me to be lucky later in my career and in my life. The GI Bill covered my college tuition, but I had to pay my living expenses and contribute money to my family while I attended school. I landed a job as a bill collector in Roxbury, a low-income community in Boston. It certainly wasn't an easy job, but it paid relatively well, and I held on to it for my entire four years at Suffolk University.

The first thing I learned at that job was to be careful—more than once I was thrown down a flight of stairs by clients who weren't happy to see the bill collector showing up at their door. I also discovered that rather than acting tough and mean and being an intimidating bully, as bill collectors in movies always do, being friendly and considerate was a much more effective approach.

The clients I visited on a daily basis tended not to be crooks and con artists. For the most part, they were poor people who just didn't have enough money to make ends meet. They took loans not to try and cheat someone or get something for nothing but to feed their families, pay for medical care, and keep a roof over their heads. They got into trouble and couldn't find any other way out. Many of them had loans all over town. These desperation loans carried sky-high interest rates that should have been illegal. But my job wasn't to change the system—it was to collect payments, and that's what I did.

When I showed up at someone's door to collect loan payments, I tried to be as friendly as I could and to get the people on my side rather than creating an adversarial relationship. I thought about how I would want to have been treated in a situation like that. I certainly understood what it was like to be poor, and I empathized with people who had no other choice but to take high-interest loans they might not be able to repay. As the saying goes, you attract more flies with honey than vinegar. So, too, you collect more bill payments with respect and friendliness than with pressure and threats. And you also get thrown down stairs less often.

In addition to helping cover my expenses while in college, my job as a bill collector helped shape the way I looked at money for the rest of my life. On graduating from Suffolk, I landed a job as an auditor at Federated Department Stores, the company that owned several chains, including Filene's, a popular department store with many locations in Boston and beyond. One of my roles at Federated was to conduct audits at various stores. I didn't particularly like working in a department store atmosphere, but I loved traveling around the United States. I had seen some of the country during my army days, when I spent time in South Carolina, Illinois, and Missouri. But the Federated job took me even farther afield, and it showed me some ways of thinking that I'd never been exposed to before.

In West Virginia, I learned about anti-Catholic prejudice, something I hadn't been exposed to growing up in Irish-Catholic Boston. One day, I rode in an elevator with four women who were shopping at the department store that I was auditing. They were talking politics and were quite affronted by the fact that a shady character by the name of John F. Kennedy had the nerve to be running for president. "Those Catholics are horrible people," I remember one of them saying. "What is this country coming to?" I was totally surprised by that comment. I knew that racial bigotry existed in the United States, but that was the first time I realized that some of that prejudice was aimed at me and my people.

Another important discovery came during a trip to Las Vegas. I'd never been to a casino, so I was excited to see the razzle-dazzle of the Vegas Strip. But I soon decided that gambling was not something I would ever do. Back then, Vegas attracted many people who really couldn't afford to be gambling. Seeing young, poor people gambling away their financial security reminded me too much of my days as a bill collector. I remember one couple in particular who had just gotten married in one of Las Vegas's many wedding chapels. As the young husband played one losing hand after another, his sobbing wife begged him to stop. "We don't have any money left!" I recall her saying. That hit me so hard, and I promised myself that I would never take up gambling. To this day, I see nothing glamorous about casinos. I was always careful with money, something I credit to that trip to Las Vegas and to my experience as a bill collector.

My time in the United States Army from 1953 to 1955 was another formative experience that helped prepare me for a successful corporate career, even though the postings I held in the army were light years away from the world of international business. The army was one of the best experiences of my life, not just because it paid for my college tuition, but because it taught me about the value of presenting myself well.

After basic training in South Carolina, I was sent to Chicago to join a unit that served as honor guards for military ceremonies and funerals. The Korean War had recently ended, and the remains of fallen American soldiers were being shipped back to the United States with some frequency. My job was to participate in ceremonies that paid tribute to these fallen soldiers upon their return to US soil. As an honor guard, I would be attired in full parade dress to create an atmosphere of profound respect and reverence. During those ceremonies, I was struck by the impact that the honor guards' presence had on the proceedings—clothes and bearing really do make the man. Having to be so completely disciplined and to keep my uniform spick-and-span perfect taught me a lot about how to present myself.

And not to make light of those serious moments, but we nattily dressed honor guards quickly figured out that the young ladies who came to those funerals were also quite impressed by our presence. After the ceremonies, we were always happy to accept invitations to the receptions sponsored by the American Legion and the Veterans of Foreign Wars. Without going into detail, I'll just say that we did our best to offer comfort to the girls at those events.

My second army posting swapped formal parade dress for a swimsuit. I had gotten close with some people in the personnel office of the Fifth Army, and they alerted me to an opening for a lifeguard at the swimming pools at Fort Leonard Wood in Missouri. I spent the second half of my army career poolside. (My children love to poke fun at me for that.) You might think that lifeguarding wouldn't have been anything more than one of the easiest posts in the army, but it actually taught me some things that helped me later on. I was a lifeguard at the officer's swimming pool, and because officers and their families were there, I had to be on my most respectful behavior at all times. Once again, I saw that the way I presented myself mattered more than where I was from or how I had grown up. I became friends with some of the families with teenage sons and daughters—I was still a teen myself—and many of them invited me to their homes for dinner. Meals were informal, and I was treated as a friend of the family rather than a private first class or a corporal. But despite that informality, I always had to remember that the man sitting at the head of the table was a colonel or higher-ranking career military officer and that I always had to conduct myself in a polite, well-mannered way.

In both of my army postings, I felt energized being surrounded by so many people who shared my goal of wanting to make something of themselves. At that time, all young men had to go into the service, but because of the GI Bill, many of the enlisted men with whom I served were poor kids like me who had joined up with the goal of doing our time in the military so we could go to college and make something of ourselves. Before the army, I had known very few college graduates or, for that matter, people who had any interest in attending college. It was very encouraging to be around so many people who, like me, felt driven to improve themselves by going to college.

Thanks to these experiences, I left the army in 1955 a far more disciplined, polished, motivated person than I had been two years earlier. It really did change my life.

I believe I could have been a success without the GI Bill and a college degree. Neither of my brothers went to college, and they both had successful careers. My older brother, John, became an entrepreneur and was smart enough to buy twenty-five Dunkin' Donut locations before the company's popularity exploded. My younger brother, Bill, was a refrigeration engineer and mechanic who bought, renovated, and sold houses along the Cape Cod coast. They have both made a very comfortable living. And now that I think about it, even though they didn't go to college, I believe they both were preparing themselves to be lucky from an early age, albeit in different ways than I was. And so did my little sister, Peggy, who raised a wonderful family despite some hard knocks early on. Although we grew up poor, our immigrant parents taught us the value of hard work and family. They were role models for us—they showed us, in their own ways, how important it was to work hard and reach for more, whether that meant a college degree, a successful career, a happy family, or a new life in a foreign land. Although I didn't always see it when I was younger, when I look back, I realize that being born into the McDonnell family of Hyde Park was probably one of my luckiest breaks of all.

THE McDONNELL FAMILY OF HYDE PARK

My sister, Peggy Malley, is the McDonnell family historian, so I've asked her to share some memories of our parents and our childhood:

Our mother, Margaret O'Neill, grew up on a farm in Eyeries in County Cork, Ireland, one of ten children. Eyeries is the most beautiful place I've ever seen, with the ocean right across the road and magnificent hills in the background. But as they say, you can't live on scenery. Times were hard in Ireland because of the Great Famine that began in the 1840s, so our mother, like millions of other poor Irish Catholics, immigrated to America in 1930 when she was twenty. She found work as a domestic, taking care of Jewish children in Brookline.

Mother was a very quiet, very tiny, very beautiful woman. Big, massive, dark sea-blue eyes and pure white skin. All four of us—my three brothers and I—have those blue eyes. Our father had them too. She just was so kind to us—so motherly, and she never yelled at us, even though she had three boys in four years and then me, the only girl and the brattiest of us all. Neither of our parents smoked or drank.

Our father, John McDonnell, was also one of ten children. He grew up on a farm in Athlone in County Roscommon—a much less scenic town than our mother's. Some of his siblings had died, moved away, or left Ireland, but because he was the youngest, he stayed behind until his mother passed away. He came to Boston in 1929, at the age of thirty.

Our parents met in 1932 at a dance at the Hibernian Hall in Roxbury, Massachusetts, where all the Irish went to socialize. They were married a year later. Our father was eleven years older than our mother, but it wasn't until long after they married that she found out he had lied about his age when they met so she wouldn't know how much older he was.

My three brothers—Johnny, Eddie, and Billy—and I were

raised as devout Catholics. We sat at the kitchen table and said the rosary every night when we were kids, and we went to church as a family every Sunday. Our father was extremely strict—when he told you something, you didn't say no or ask him why. You just did it. If the boys were hanging around on the corner, he'd go down and tell them to come home. We had a huge garden in our backyard in Hyde Park, where we grew every kind of vegetable. We ate really well thanks to that garden. Our father made us do chores, and we did them obediently. And he expected us to do our homework perfectly. He worked nights, and if our homework wasn't done when he got home, he would wake us up to go down to the dining room table to do it properly. But even though he was strict, we respected him. Our upbringing didn't do us any harm.

As a family, we danced to Irish music in our living room every Sunday afternoon. All four of us kids were fantastic dancers. After the dancing, we would go roller-skating at Chez-Vous, a roller rink in Dorchester. Our parents made my brothers take me along. That was the deal—if they wanted to go, they had to take their little sister. But they didn't mind.

Our father did all kinds of work around the Boston area. He made a fairly good salary early on for an Irish immigrant— maybe $5 or $10 a week. We had a nice humble home that we were brought up in, a six-room house in Hyde Park. We were so fortunate to be brought up with the parents that we had and to live in the house that we had, which was brand new back then.

My brothers were even stricter than our father, and Eddie was the worst of all. (Even at this age, I still call him Eddie.) He didn't want me to go out of the house until I was sixteen. Eddie was the smartest one. We used to say to our mother, "Ma, you were supposed to give all of us brains, not just Eddie. You were supposed to pass them around." And she'd say, "You're all fine."

I don't remember my brothers ever fighting. That's unusual for three brothers. But it's the way we were brought up. You respected one another. Maybe you said things under your breath, but no fighting. That's true even to this day. I'm lucky I still have all three brothers alive and in pretty good health. And we all get along.

When our mother was in her sixties, my daughters and I took her back to Ireland for the first time since she came over forty-six years earlier. She always wanted to go back, but our father never did—too many sad memories for him, he said. He died at sixty-three of a massive heart attack. Back then I thought he was so old when he died, but I realize now he wasn't old at all. My mother lived to eighty-eight.

We're all immensely proud of Eddie. My mother, being Irish, would always worry about him and his family off living in Brazil or England or wherever. But she was proud of him. He knew what he wanted in life, and he wasn't going to settle for anything but the best. But success hasn't changed him—he's the same now as he was when we were children. He's always been himself.

2

STEP OUT OF YOUR COMFORT ZONE

WHEN GEORGE BREMSER JR., THE PRESIDENT OF GENERAL FOODS, TOLD ME THAT HE WANTED TO SEND ME TO BRAZIL TO WORK AT KIBON IN 1968, I DIDN'T SAY YES RIGHT AWAY. At first, all I could think of were the roadblocks: I didn't know how to speak Portuguese. I knew nothing about the Brazilian culture. Working in Brazil would require me and my family to relocate to a South American country we knew little about. On the business side, Kibon had numerous problems, not the least of which was that it was poorly run and hemorrhaging money. Certainly it had potential. Kibon, which had been founded in the 1940s and acquired by General Foods in the early 1960s, was the biggest ice cream producer in Brazil, and even though it wasn't making money for General Foods, I was sure there was plenty of room to grow the company's market share and expand its product development program. But moving from White Plains, New York, to São Paulo, Brazil, would be a huge step out of my comfort zone.

Thankfully, I didn't let that initial hesitation stop me from accepting this incredible opportunity. I wanted to live in a different world than the one in which I'd been raised. Not that there is anything wrong with staying put, but I wanted an entirely different experience than that. I wanted to get out of my comfort zone—my educational comfort zone, my cultural comfort zone, my geographic comfort zone. And I'm so glad I did, because doing so has given me an incredibly rewarding life.

It's not always easy to get out of your comfort zone. It certainly wasn't for me—after I finished high school, my parents and many of the people around me simply couldn't understand why I would want to go to college when I could get a blue-collar job in my neighborhood. Back then, I wasn't even sure what I wanted, but I knew I wanted something more, something different. Others questioned my choices, but I had to be true to myself, even when it meant going off in a direction that perplexed my family and friends.

When I completed my army service in 1955, I enrolled at Suffolk University. I decided to study business because that major made the most sense. I didn't have grandiose dreams about becoming a doctor or anything like that. All I knew was that I had to major in something that would qualify me for a good job when I finished. I was good at math, so I chose business administration.

Remember I mentioned that the first time I ever saw my father cry was when I told him I planned to go into the army so I could get the GI Bill and then go to college? Well, the second time I saw him cry was when I graduated from Suffolk. He was so proud, even if he didn't understand my desire to pursue a different life than his. Too bad he didn't live long enough to see me receive an honorary doctorate from Suffolk University in 1984.

I aspired to being more than just a lace-curtain Irishman in Boston. Like so many children of Irish immigrants at the time, I grew up hearing all about the so-called evolution of the Irish in America. It was standard propaganda in my neighborhood. The poorest were known as shanty Irish because they lived in shanties without plumbing. The equivalent of this in my Boston neighborhood meant living in a tenement with six families on one floor, all of whom shared one toilet. Those who moved up a bit in the world became a one-toilet Irish family, meaning they were lucky enough to have an apartment or even a house with one toilet. The really fortunate families had two toilets, as my family eventually did. Those who earned enough to put lace curtains on their windows were—you guessed it—lace-curtain Irish. These were all stereotypes, of course, but many of the people I knew bought into them. I remember how proud my father was when he installed a second bathroom in the basement of our house. With that, we had become two-toilet Irish. It was a big achievement, but I wanted more than that.

I graduated from Suffolk in June of 1959 and married my college sweetheart, Catherine (Kay) McNamara, a month later. I'd found love, but finding a job was a bit harder. While I was searching, I asked my future brother-in-law—the fellow who was about to marry Kay's sister—for advice. He was attending Harvard Business School, and I thought he might have some tips for me. I told him I was checking the job listings in the *Wall Street Journal* and the *New York Times*. "Where else should I look?" I asked him. I'll never forget his response.

"Ed, don't kid yourself," he said. "You're not going to get anywhere with a degree from Suffolk University. You have no chance of getting a good job, so don't even bother trying." That really teed me off; although I have to admit, it also fired me up. I'd show him what a Suffolk grad could do.

Kay was a wonderful woman, but her family didn't think much of me. My father-in-law, Albert, owned J. H. McNamara Concrete, which at the time was the second biggest concrete company in Massachusetts. Kay's family was affluent, with a big house in Allston, Massachusetts, and a beach house in Scituate, a prosperous town along the shore between

Boston and Cape Cod. Kay's father felt that all of his daughters except Kay had married well. He didn't like me because, in his opinion, I came from nothing, I had nothing, I knew nothing, and I would amount to nothing. In his eyes, I was a failure in life before I'd ever really gotten started.

As it turned out, though, I knew more about business than Albert McNamara realized. He mentioned to me one day around the time Kay and I were to marry that he had a chance to invest in a pro sports team that was being formed in Boston. He and a few other construction executives had been offered an opportunity to get in on the ground floor of this deal. I don't remember the exact numbers, but for an investment of something in the neighborhood of $30,000, he could have owned about 10 percent of this new team. I thought it was a fantastic deal, and I pushed him to make the investment. "You'd be crazy not to do this!" I said. "Walking away from this opportunity would be the most insane thing you could ever do!"

But Mr. McNamara felt he knew better, and he wasn't about to take my advice. "Kid, you don't know what the hell you're talking about," he told me. But it turned out my instincts were pretty good. Can you imagine what 10 percent of the New England Patriots is worth today?

● ● ●

I soon found a job working as an auditor for Federated Department Stores. Federated interviewed me at Suffolk University and was one of the only companies that offered me a job. Being an auditor for Federated Department Stores certainly didn't impress my in-laws, but I was excited to be going to New York to begin my career. I flew from Boston to New York City—I think the fare was about $18—and I arrived in New York with just a few dollars in my pocket. I planned to stay at the YMCA in Midtown for $3 a night. I hailed a cab and told the cabbie I was headed for the YMCA.

The fare was $5.90, and I had $6. When we arrived at the Y, I gave my $6 to the cabbie and told him to keep the change. But he gave the tip back to me and said, "Kid, you need this money more than I do." And he was right. I always respected cab drivers after that.

Federated sent me around the country to audit various stores. I learned a lot during my two years at Federated, but I figured out pretty quickly that I didn't want to stay in the retail business. So when I heard that Raytheon was hiring auditors, I submitted an application and was hired.

At the time, Raytheon was heavily involved in developing missile guidance systems. I was no more interested in missiles than I was in department stores, but it seemed like a step up. I'm so very glad I took that job—it turned out to be one of the best breaks of my career because it gave me my first exposure to international living. I started working in Raytheon's location in Lexington, Massachusetts, which was fine; but after a couple of years, the company sent me and my family to London for a year. Raytheon was acquiring a company in England, and I was posted in London as a junior member of the acquisitions team. When my manager at Raytheon told me they wanted me to go to London, I was so excited. I couldn't believe my good luck.

My job as an auditor on the Raytheon acquisitions team was to chase down all the financial details about the corporation we wanted to take over. When a company is being acquired, its owners and managers tend to want to puff up the financials to make them look better than they really are, but my team and I were there to push aside the bull and get to the real numbers. Learning how to do this was a skill that would serve me well later in my career when I was in charge of acquiring companies around the world.

During my Raytheon days, I discovered that I was a pretty good number cruncher. But I also realized fairly early on that I didn't want to stay with auditing forever. Numbers didn't capture my attention as they did with some of my auditing peers. I was much more interested in what was behind the numbers—what they meant for a business and the stories they told about the big picture for a company or a market.

I continued working as an auditor for a few more years before leaving it behind, but looking back, I see that being an auditor was a tremendous help to me throughout my career. It taught me how to read financial statements and understand whether a business was—or had the potential to be—successful. I didn't have to rely only on explanations from others; auditing gave me the ability to understand the numbers on my own, which is something that many business leaders don't know how to do. I initiated and was involved in many corporate acquisitions over the years, and having a background in auditing served me very well as I decided which companies to acquire and which deals to ignore. You could say that being an auditor was yet another way that I prepared myself to be lucky.

Living in London was wonderful. I loved living overseas, being exposed to a different culture than the one I'd grown up in, and getting to know so many interesting people. Despite what I'd always heard about British people and their stiff upper lips, I actually found them to be quite warm. One of my most poignant memories of living in London is the weekend that President John F. Kennedy was assassinated. The British people loved JFK and the Kennedy family. Back in the late 1930s, when JFK was a college student, his father, Joe Kennedy, was appointed US ambassador to Great Britain. When the new ambassador and his large family arrived in London, they took the country by storm, winning the hearts of every station of British society, from commoners all the way up to the monarchy. Joe Kennedy's standing in the eyes of the British people fell when he backed the appeasement of Hitler and argued against the United States providing aid to Britain during World War II, but the British people never stopped loving JFK.

Much to my surprise, that love carried over to my family and me.

Shortly after the news broke of Kennedy's assassination on November 22, 1963, food, gifts, flowers, and sympathy cards started to show up at the home in which my family and I lived in London. My coworkers, our neighbors, and even nearby shopkeepers showered us with condolences for President Kennedy's death. They wanted to comfort us, but I think even more importantly, they needed to express their own sadness at the loss of this great man. It was an incredibly touching experience.

To say that my time working for Raytheon in London changed my life is to make the greatest of understatements. I enjoyed the hell out of living in London, even though most of the work I was doing for the acquisition team was grunt work. We worked hard and we played hard. I liked it so much that when my assignment came to an end, I decided to search for a job that would allow me to have more opportunities to work abroad. Even though they had sent me to London for a year, overseas assignments weren't typical at Raytheon, and staying with that company would mean living in the States. Once I had a taste of international living, I didn't want to give it up.

I found the job I was looking for at General Foods, which had more of an international presence than Raytheon. I was happy to accept a job as a financial analyst because I knew there was a potential for me to work overseas. My time in London helped me clarify my most important career goal: to work in international business. To put it plainly, I wanted to be an internationalist. And moving to General Foods was my best next step toward achieving that goal. I took the job at General Foods, and within two years, I was working at Kibon in Brazil.

• • •

One of the first tasks I set for myself after General Foods sent me to São Paulo was to learn Portuguese. A weakness I had observed among the previous top managers at Kibon, all of whom were sent to Brazil from General Foods' offices in Europe or the United States, was that they didn't seem to make the effort to understand the mindset of the Brazilian people who worked at the company—what drove them, what motivated them. Kibon employed 4,600 people, but the previous managers seemed unable to bring out the best in these employees. I believed that if I could immerse myself in Brazilian culture and the Brazilian perspective in a way that other managers had not, I would discover how to motivate the workers and improve Kibon's performance.

Hardly anyone at Kibon spoke English, and although I was assigned an interpreter, I knew that I'd have a far better chance of connecting with the Brazilians in the company if I made a strong effort to learn their language. I hired an instructor to teach me Portuguese from 7 a.m. to 8 a.m. every day, an hour before the workday started. Although I never became fluent in Portuguese, I did learn enough to speak and understand far more than I would have without those daily lessons. My children, on the other hand, soaked up the language as only children can—especially my youngest, Beth, who was just a toddler at the time. All three of them could soon speak Portuguese like native-born Brazilians.

The way in which Kibon employees supported my halting attempts to speak to them in their language told me so much about them. They were very supportive of me and enjoyed helping me. Having spent some time in Paris, I knew what it was like to be scorned for being an imperfect speaker of a language. I remember Parisians being insulted when I tried to speak to them with my less-than-perfect French. But the Brazilians were so patient, and I felt such warmth and appreciation toward them for welcoming me despite the fact that I was butchering their language as I attempted to speak to them. For them, my wanting to communicate to them in their language was a sign of respect. It showed them that I was different from the managers who had come before me. Just as I had learned when I was a bill collector that treating people with respect is much more effective than bullying them, I discovered that once the Kibon employees realized that I respected them, a fundamental change began to occur in the company.

Learning the language was just a first step, but it showed the Kibon employees that I wasn't like the other European and American managers who had come to Brazil for the standard two-year stint simply to have a good time and add an international experience to their résumés. Within a couple of years, the company began to turn a profit, and by the time I left Kibon eight years later, it had grown into a big success for General Foods.

Obviously, there is much more to this success story than my learning Portuguese. My team and I brought about many changes at Kibon. Our key objective was to introduce as many new grocery products as possible to the Brazilian market. But I don't think any of those changes or product development plans would have been successful without the decision to step out of my comfort zone, immerse myself in the company and in the Brazilian culture, and commit fully to the Brazilian Kibon family both personally and professionally. Through the years, I've assigned many businesspeople to international postings, and without exception, the most successful ones were those who devoted themselves to becoming part of the culture in which they were living and working. They didn't just step out of their comfort zone; they fully inhabited and embraced the new world into which they had stepped. Doing this isn't always easy—believe me, learning Portuguese as an adult was a hell of a challenge. But from my view, it is always worth the effort.

Of course, being an outsider can sometimes convey business advantages because you have the ability to look at things a little differently than everyone else. I have a good story about this, but I'll let my friend Fernando Kfouri tell it:

Ed was a real gringo when he came down to Brazil. He had no real international experience, and here he was coming to a country with hyperinflation and difficult accounting. It wasn't easy. But he had street smarts.

Here's an example of how he brought a different perspective to the business. The ice cream business in Brazil was primarily novelty items like Popsicles, Eskimo Pies, and so on. All impulse items. These required very good distribution, which meant having ice cream freezers in many, many locations. Kibon used to own the ice cream freezers it installed in retail stores. Because these freezers were Kibon's property, retailers could only have Kibon ice cream in them. But sometimes we would find non-Kibon products in a freezer, and when this happened repeatedly, we would penalize the retailer by taking away our freezer.

At one point, a new competitor came up with a strategy of selling its coolers to the retailers. When a retailer bought their own cooler, they could put whatever they wanted in it. Ed saw an opportunity to turn this to Kibon's advantage, and he personally led a blitzkrieg-type action. One Christmas Eve, he sent out an army of Kibon employees to paint the competitor's freezers with Kibon colors and replace all the competitor's products with Kibon products. This operation, which was planned carefully with the retailers, started late in the afternoon and was finished by the time the stores closed. As a result, Kibon took 20 percent of the market share from the competitor. The competitor's general manager was fired a few days later. A Brazilian wouldn't have done that—but Ed, a gringo with street smarts, did.

Call it serendipity. Just as I was discovering my fascination with international business, the world of international commerce was undergoing one of the most dramatic changes in history. When I started out, most companies based in the United States focused mainly on their domestic business. They may have had a small international presence, but overseas business was unlikely to contribute much to their bottom lines. Take General Foods as an example: we did have some international holdings, like Kibon, but they were just a tiny part of the corporate portfolio. And when I joined Seagram in 1981, almost all of the company's profits came from North America; by the time I retired in 1995, 80 percent of Seagram profits came from outside North America. Almost every company today is intensely global, but back in the 1960s, '70s, and even into the early '80s, most US companies paid attention primarily to their own backyard. The rest of the world was an afterthought. But that was starting to change around the time my career began.

To give you some idea of what was going on in the world at that time, I'll turn to my good friend Bill O'Neill Jr., who recently retired as dean of the Sawyer Business School at Suffolk University. Here's his perspective:

World War II had ended in 1945, but it took years for countries involved in the war to recuperate economically. That recovery strengthened in the 1960s and 1970s, especially in countries such as France, Germany, England, and Japan. As countries finally started having more money to spend, living standards went up, and demand for consumer products skyrocketed. At that point, the United States had the dominant economy in the world. No other country even came close.

As US companies started to see market opportunities in other countries, they began expanding by acquiring foreign companies, building factories, expanding full operations, and growing their presence overseas. It wasn't just a one-way street—overseas companies, such as those in the auto industry and consumer electronics, were sending their products into the United States as well.

Several other factors contributed to the growth of international business during this time as well. Tariffs came down. Giant new markets opened up around the world, especially in Asia. And as more people around the world gained access to American television shows and advertisements, their desire for American consumer goods exploded.

And I was in the middle of all that. Just as globalism was transforming world markets, I was climbing corporate ladders, looking for opportunities to live and work overseas.

Bill O'Neill's career trajectory parallels mine somewhat. Although we never worked together, we oversaw similar overseas expansions in different markets. After a stint at Ford Motor Company early in his career, Bill spent many years at the Polaroid Corporation, playing an important part in that company's global growth. When he first joined Polaroid in 1970, it had a tiny international presence, but within ten years, global business grew to be the largest contributor to the company's profits. The same was true of Seagram, where I led international operations in the 1980s and '90s.

For many United States–based executives, globalism was not a completely welcome change. Yes, they wanted to see their companies' financials improve and their companies rise in international prominence. But quite a few of them had no interest in packing their trunks and moving to new profit centers like South America or Asia or even Europe. Rather than stepping out of their American comfort zone, they wanted to stay in the places in which they'd grown up. Or if they did go overseas, they were likely to treat their international posting like the managers who preceded me at Kibon, living there but not really engaging with the country or the culture. Bill O'Neill tells a story about his Polaroid days, when he flew over to Hong Kong to meet with an American whom he had sent over to run the company's Asia operations. When lunchtime rolled around, Bill invited this manager to his favorite Chinese restaurant, but the manager declined to go because—are you ready for this?—he didn't like Chinese food and would only eat lunch at McDonald's. That is the worst example I've ever heard of not being able to step out of one's comfort zone.

Another example involves a very wealthy man I met in the mid-1970s when I lived in Minnesota. I had recently taken a position with Pillsbury, and the company chairman threw a party to introduce me to the upper echelon of Minneapolis society, including the heir to a large midwestern department store chain. As we chatted, this fellow told me how lucky I was to have lived in England and Brazil. "I wish I could do that," he said.

"Of course you can," I said. "You're a billionaire. You can do whatever you want, live wherever you want, buy a home wherever you want." But he was talking about stepping out of his Minneapolis comfort zone and accepting his family's expectation that he stay home and run the family business. I still remember how regretful he looked when he told me that he had no choice but to commit himself to Minnesota. I am so grateful that I found the courage to break out of the lifestyle I had grown up with.

As my old friend and Seagram colleague James Espey says, "Not to be critical, but too many Americans think the world begins in San Francisco and ends in New York. But it doesn't. To succeed in business today, you have to look outward, not inward."

Fortunately, the reluctance of other executives to accept overseas postings only helped me. When I started out, I had more breaks than the average person because at that time, living overseas and working in international divisions of American companies wasn't something that many people wanted to take on. If anything, it was seen as a dead end or a detour from the traditional rise to corporate success. But to me, working internationally seemed much more exciting than staying home. Today, of course, there's far more of an appreciation of the benefits of living internationally, both in terms of propelling a career forward and having fascinating life experiences. Indeed, getting out of your comfort zone can provide opportunities for advancement you might not have if you stay close to home.

● ● ●

I never forgot how instrumental the GI Bill was in helping me get out of the comfort zone in which I was raised. And so, many years ago when Bill O'Neill approached me about creating a scholarship program at Suffolk University, I knew exactly how I wanted to structure it: as a way to help college students, especially children of immigrants and first-generation college students, step out of their comfort zones and have international experiences. I wanted to open a door to give these students some kind of access to the world.

Students with the means to do so can learn about other cultures during a summer or semester abroad. But that's not an option for many lower-income students who have to hold down jobs during college and summer breaks—like I did, back when I was a bill collector. I funded the McDonnell Scholars Program because I don't want hardworking students like these to miss out on an international experience just because they can't afford to travel or take time off from the jobs that are allowing them to pay for their educations. The McDonnell scholarships at Suffolk help about a dozen students per year participate in a seven- to ten-day global learning experience. Bill O'Neill sums up what these trips do for the McDonnell Scholars:

We want students to go to a country where the food is different, the clothing is different, the languages are different, and the culture is different. We put them in corporations, give them projects to work on, and require them to make reports. They have to assimilate in a relatively short period of time so they can do business in another country, just as they would have to on a business trip. It's an eye-opener for these students, many of whom have never traveled internationally, because they learn to approach issues in a different way. If they don't know how to do this, they're at a disadvantage.

Marisa Kelly, Suffolk University's president, adds:

Sometimes these students have never been out of New England or have never been on a plane before. Just the experience of traveling itself is significant. But in the case of the McDonnell Scholars Program, they're combining the opportunity to have global exposure with concrete international business opportunities, networking, talking with successful business leaders in other countries, and learning about international business. It's really incredibly rewarding for them.

In other words, these students have a chance to see what it takes to navigate business and life outside of their comfort zone.

One of Suffolk's missions is to make education accessible to all kinds of students—not just wealthy kids raised by parents with successful business careers. But it's not just up to colleges to help these kids—we all have to contribute to the effort of preparing them to make their way in the world. President Kelly puts it this way: "Despite our best efforts as an institution to provide them with scholarships and financial aid of various sorts, taking advantage of international opportunities is, for some of them, just out of reach. But thanks to donors like Ed, we are able to fund those experiences for students."

I'd be remiss if I didn't mention that in addition to his skills in international business and leading a top business school, Bill O'Neill had an astonishing ability to squeeze money out of people for his students. I recall a number of times when he'd come down to New York and have lunch with me at the Four Seasons. He'd sit down and say to me, "I need at least $25,000 from you today, and I'm not leaving until I get it." He always got it—and I'd end up paying for lunch too. The students at Suffolk's Sawyer Business School were lucky to have him. And they're lucky to attend a school that puts such an emphasis on international experiences for business students.

As adults, all of my children stepped out of their comfort zones and pursued careers that sent them around the world. Ted, my eldest, who launched his career at Seagram and now runs his own premium spirits agency and industry consulting firm, has lived in various countries in the Asia-Pacific area. My middle child, Paul, who also works in the liquor industry, ran one of my businesses in the US Virgin Islands. And Beth, my youngest, traveled the world in the Up with People performing arts program in addition to working at a destination management company in the US Virgin Islands for several years. "Living internationally in a culture that is not your own is a cool thing to do," Beth says. "And now, because of the lives we've lived, we have friends all around the world. When you hear about something happening in London or Brazil or the Virgin Islands, it's not just a foreign idea. Those are places I've lived—they were home for a while. It really does make the world a smaller place."

Living and working abroad has enriched my life and given me decades of wonderful opportunities. I am so thankful to have had the chance to experience other countries and immerse myself in other cultures. Stepping out of my comfort zone made all the difference for me and allowed me to have a life I couldn't even have dreamed of when I was growing up. Once you start leaving your comfort zone, you just never know what exciting places your life will take you.

WORTH THE RISK

My nephew John McDonnell launched his career at Seagram and then became COO and president of International at the Patrón Spirits Company, where he led the company's US, international, and duty-free expansion. Currently, John is the managing director of International at Tito's "Handmade" Vodka. Here's how John, who, like me, grew up in Boston, feels about getting out of his comfort zone.

I have a lot in common with Ed. Like him, I was raised in Hyde Park. I grew up in the same house he grew up in. I went to the same grammar school as Ed for a year. I spent many of my summers with his mother (my grandmother), who watched me while my parents worked. And I went to Suffolk University, Ed's alma mater. We have a unique relationship because we grew up in the same world.

At my college graduation, Ed asked me if I had a job lined up. I had been running a political campaign for Tom Menino, a fellow Hyde Park resident who eventually became the longest-serving mayor of Boston, but I was looking for a job in business. "Where are you going to work?" Ed asked me.

"You're going to give me a job," I joked—but as it turned out, that's exactly what happened. Ed introduced me to someone at Seagram, I went for an interview, and I was hired for a job in marketing research. Thanks to Ed I've had a long, enjoyable career in the liquor industry. My family and I moved fifteen times in twenty-five years, chasing promotions and getting ahead. And I owe it all to Ed, who got me my big break.

Most people in the liquor industry would credit Ed with building Seagram globally. I learned a lot watching what he did, and I applied a great deal of it when I went to work at the Patrón Spirits Company, where my team and I grew revenue from $75 million to $600 million in part by expanding our global business. And now I'm doing that at Tito's "Handmade," where we're growing the worldwide market by innovating our strategic planning, routes to market, and marketing. There are a lot of similarities between what Ed did and what I'm doing.

When I was first getting established, Ed told me that if I wanted to be successful in the liquor business, I had to go international, because that's how you really learn to run a business. And he was 100 percent right. When I worked in the United States, my job really was babysitting liquor distributors. But when I went overseas, I was running the entire business, soup to nuts—all disciplines, including sales, marketing, logistics, pricing, contracts, and trademark protection. I was responsible for everything. The challenges I faced were significantly greater, but the rewards were greater, too.

Here's a simple example: In the United States, the financials are all done in US dollars. But as the head of international business, I'm thinking about all of the currencies in the area I'm responsible for. Every morning when I wake up, I wonder, did the dollar go up? Did the dollar go down? Is the yen stronger? Is the euro weaker? Those fluctuations change your pricing all the time. Constantly. You can't manage currencies, but you have to protect the brand integrity. So it's much more complex, but it's also more satisfying. Ed told me to get out of my comfort zone and take risks, and I'm glad I did.

3

DO THE RIGHT THING

MY PARENTS RAISED ME WITH A STRONG SENSE OF RIGHT AND WRONG. Some of this came from their devout Catholic faith, but my sense is that they both would have been ethical people no matter what their religion. They taught my brothers and sister and me to do the right thing, and it was a lesson I tried to carry with me throughout my business career. I certainly wasn't 100 percent successful in my efforts to do right, but I always considered it a value I wanted to honor, and I felt unhappy with myself when I fell short.

One of my favorite stories about doing the right thing comes from my early days at Kibon. It demonstrates something that I've seen many times over the years. Obviously, doing right is right because it benefits the person or people at whom the action is directed. But it often delivers unexpected rewards to the individual who is choosing to act honorably.

During my first two years at Kibon in São Paulo, my team and I made some positive progress toward turning the company around, but we were still losing money. Although we were doing whatever we could think of to boost profitability, we couldn't quite figure out how to bring about the changes needed to improve the company's bottom line significantly. Around that time, I had a meeting with Fernando, my director of human resources. (This is a different Fernando than Fernando Kfouri, who worked with me for many years at Kibon and, later, at Seagram.) After discussing whatever topics needed attention, I could tell he still had something on his mind.

"What is it, Fernando?" I asked. After hesitating a bit, he spoke up.

"Señor McDonnell, I have a suggestion," Fernando said. "As you know, Brazil is in the World Cup finals next week. I propose that if we win the World Cup, everyone who works for Kibon gets a week off with pay."

I couldn't believe my ears. A paid week off for 4,600 people?

"Are you out of your mind, Fernando?" I asked. I trusted this man, but at this moment, I believed he was suffering from a bout of temporary insanity. "We're losing money every day, and you want me to pay everyone in the entire company to take a week off? What in the world could you possibly be thinking?"

But when I listened to his response, I realized it made complete sense.

"You know how popular soccer is in Brazil," Fernando said, although of course he called it *futebol*—football—and not soccer. I certainly did know that. Even though I, like most Americans in 1970, wasn't much of a soccer fan, I appreciated how much Brazilians loved the game and how deeply they adored Pelé, the star of the Brazilian team and the greatest soccer player of all time. There are no words to describe how passionate Brazilians were about soccer and Pelé.

"If we win the World Cup," Fernando explained, "everyone will go wild! They'll be so happy they'll want to take the week off to celebrate. And if they don't receive their wages for a week, they'll be very upset. But if you pay them, they'll love you for it."

I thought about it for a moment and realized that Fernando had an excellent point. Giving the workers paid time off was the right thing to do because going without pay for a week would be a hardship for most of them. But it was also an opportunity for me to show the workers some respect and perhaps even to earn their respect as well.

Financially it would be a risk to give everyone a paid week off. But Fernando believed it would be a risk that would pay off.

"Okay, you've convinced me," I told Fernando. We wrote a memo announcing the decision and distributed it to all of the employees the next day. They were overjoyed.

As expected, the great Pelé led the Brazilian team to a World Cup victory with an exciting tournament. The Kibon factory shut down, the entire country celebrated like crazy, and our employees received their pay for the week.

Then, when they returned to work, something amazing began to happen. Ideas began pouring in from employees about ways to improve productivity throughout the company. Workers on the factory floor made suggestions about updating equipment to make it more cost-effective. Production people recommended updates to some of our processes to streamline operating procedures. Salespeople came up with ways to expand our presence in shops and markets. Everyone in the company had known we were trying to turn Kibon around and make it profitable, but before the World Cup, most of the employees hadn't really invested themselves in the effort to make improvements. Now, for the first time, the entire workforce seemed to be pulling together to turn the ship around. They felt motivated, and once they saw that their suggestions were being heard and implemented, they offered even more advice. After I showed the workers that I supported something that was intensely important to them, they returned the favor by supporting something that was intensely important to *me*.

What an impact those employees had on Kibon's success! By the end of the year, the company was starting to turn a profit.

In addition to ice cream, Kibon produced other General Foods products for the Brazilian market, including things like Maxwell House coffee and Jell-O gelatin. Previously, these types of products hadn't been available in Brazil, but supermarkets were just starting to appear, and Kibon was helping to fill them with American-style products that intrigued Brazilian shoppers. But it wasn't enough just to be manufacturing these products—we had to do it in an efficient, profitable way. The employee suggestions that flowed in after the World Cup win turned the company around. During the following couple of years, revenues continued to grow, and by the time I left Kibon, it was one of the most successful international holdings in the General Foods family. It was as decisive a victory for Kibon as it had been for Pelé and the Brazilian *futebol* team.

ALWAYS TIME FOR CAKE

Sonia Uzun Tenorio was my trusted assistant at Kibon. I asked her to share some memories about our days working together in Brazil.

I worked as a secretary at Kibon for thirty years, but I had only been there a couple of years when Ed McDonnell arrived. I quickly noticed that he was different from the other general managers before him. One of them in particular was a very rude, cold guy whom everyone disliked. But when Ed came, things changed because he was a people person with a very good sense of humor. That made a big difference to everyone.

It was nicer to be there after Ed arrived. He was a party guy who attended every celebration of the company. We used to have, for instance, Truck Drivers' Day. The drivers would have a cake, and there was Ed, celebrating with them. If it was somebody's birthday, there was Ed. He went to everything but baby showers, and the only reason he didn't go to them was that he was not invited.

People at all levels—directors, management, workers, everybody—responded to the way Ed treated them by being more loyal, more committed, and more enthusiastic. It was good to see him even on Saturdays or Sunday mornings at the platform where the trucks left, full of ice cream. I don't know what he did for the profits of the company or how much market share he stole from the competition. I only know that he made a difference in many people's lives.

I remember once, one of the secretaries bought $20,000 in US dollars that turned out to be counterfeit. She bought them for an uncle, and when she found out they were fake, she was so upset. Ed wanted to help her, but he didn't know what to do. Then he figured out a plan. Here in Brazil, we have a fund that companies have to make deposits into every month. Then if they fire you, you can withdraw some of the money. Ed figured out a way to let her withdraw some of the money and use it to repay her uncle. It was a great help to her.

Ed tells everyone that when I worked for him, I couldn't speak a word of English and that he taught me English. And I would say, sure, listen to my Irish accent. He was always making jokes. Very irreverent.

I was twenty-one years old when I started working for Ed, and

I learned many important things from him. I picked up a little bit of his irreverent style and learned not to be afraid of people in high positions. I became a very secure person, comfortable with all kinds of people, which was good, because I worked with eight general managers over the years—American, French, German, Brazilian.

Ed was a very good president, and the company did well with him. But that's not what people remember about him. They remember Ed—the nice person, the good sense of humor. Sometimes he got very upset, very uptight, but he had a good heart. We worked very hard, but it was fun. After Ed left, I missed him a lot.

The more profits increased at Kibon, the more we were able to give back to the employees. The late 1960s and early 1970s were very tough times in Brazil, and many people lacked access to medical care. The company did the right thing and set up medical clinics and maternity wards so the employees could see doctors when they needed to. We also provided a nursery for workers' children.

"It was completely unusual for a company to have a clinic and a nursery—other companies didn't have them," recalls Sonia Uzun Tenorio, who was not only my secretary at Kibon but also a close friend to our family. "It was something very special at Kibon. We all loved the nursery. From my office, I could see the babies lying in the grass, catching some sun. We used to say that the best products made at Kibon were the babies."

It was important to me that the Kibon workers received medical care at work because the vast majority of them earned minimum wage, and medical care was expensive. This was a way for us to treat those employees with respect, help them stay healthy, and give something back to them for their hard work and commitment to General Foods. Having come from very little myself, I knew that expenses like an unexpected medical bill could throw a struggling family off course for years. Many of the people I had visited as a bill collector had gone into debt paying for medical care for their families. And I admit, there's a business benefit as well: a healthy workforce can do more for a company than workers who are worried about medical problems with themselves or their families. It just makes sense on so many levels to do the right thing and take good care of the people who work for you.

Having company-provided health care drew the best people to Kibon. Our wages were similar to those paid by other companies, but benefits such as on-site medical clinics and maternity care made people want to work at Kibon. Other companies didn't have clinics and nurseries. Thanks to benefits like these, employees said they felt like they were part of the Kibon family, and that meant something to them. They showed their appreciation with loyalty and hard work. It definitely was a situation where doing the right thing helped everyone.

I loved the people I worked with at Kibon. They were so warm and friendly, and they made me and my family feel so welcome. It has always been my policy to treat employees with respect, but that was easy to do with the people at Kibon. Over the years, I have often felt astonished to witness the lack of respect practiced by some executives, especially those who worked internationally for the first time. Too many Americans and Europeans adopt what I can only describe as a colonial mentality, one that is based on a sense of cultural superiority that I find not only appalling but completely unsupportive of business success. What sense does it make to go to another country and treat the people who live and work there as if they don't understand their own world? Why not respect their knowledge and experience and work with them as a team? Whenever I would go to a new overseas posting, I would put myself in the shoes of the people working there. I would want to be treated with respect, to have an opportunity to share my knowledge and contribute to the company's success, to receive opportunities for professional growth and promotion, and I just assumed that the people I worked with wanted all of those things, too. Disrespecting them wouldn't help them, and it certainly wouldn't make things any better for me or the company. Rather than feel threatened by their accomplishments and brilliant ideas, as some executives did, I felt happy to see them prosper. Their success benefited the company and made me look good, too.

● ● ●

My belief in doing the right thing shaped how I worked at all my jobs, from General Foods to Pillsbury to Seagram and beyond. It affected how I looked at other people and influenced me as I made hiring decisions. A specific example of this is Tony Rodriguez, who worked at Seagram when I was brought on to head the international division of the company. When I first encountered Tony, he was working on Seagram's corporate planning side, which had the job of reviewing and assessing the plans of new international businesses. I'll let him take it from here:

> The first time I met Ed, it was under tense circumstances. I had recently written a critical review of one of his international affiliates, which had taken action to do what we used to call "loading the trade" to make their sales numbers look good. At least, that was my analysis of the situation. After I wrote it up in the quarterly review of the international businesses, I got a call from the office of the mighty Ed McDonnell, who I had heard was kind of an "Irish thug."
>
> And I was sure I wasn't being summoned to his office for a good reason. Incidentally, these were the circumstances under

which many people met Ed. When he was unhappy with something that you'd done, he let you know about it personally. So he and his chief finance guy, John Griffin, another "Irish thug," brought me in and asked me to explain why I wrote what I did about the affiliate. And I thought, crap, I need this like a hole in the head. But I had done my homework, and I was sure that the affiliate had loaded the trade.

Ed was a great poker player who never showed his cards. He wasn't emotional or harsh. He just asked me to explain my side of the story. So I gave him the facts behind what I wrote and an explanation of how I came to the conclusions. And then I said, "If there's something here that is inaccurate, or if I've missed something, I'll correct it or issue a retraction. But I'm trying to be an honorable person and do what's right."

I expected him to argue with me or try to convince me that I'd come to the wrong conclusion or that I should cover up my findings. But he didn't. Instead, he just looked me in the eye and said, "Tony, everything you said is totally right, which is why I want you to come work for me on the international team."

Talk about surprise. I thought he was going to try to get me fired, not try to move me onto his team. But he told me he was impressed with what I had done and that I'd stood up for myself and my work. And he said, "You're the kind of person I want working for me, someone who will stand up to me, not an ass-kisser who's going to do whatever I want." And it turned out to be true—Ed really was looking for people with integrity who would tell him what he needed to hear. He didn't always like it, and he didn't always act on it, but he would always listen to you.

Tony is absolutely right. I never wanted to work with people who would leave their integrity at the door and say anything just to get the boss to like them. And I had no respect for bosses who would only listen to people who flattered them and agreed with them on everything. If I'd done that, I never would have been successful. I never believed that I was the only one with the right answers.

There were many other times when Tony helped me do the right thing. An example that stands out is when Judy Goldfarb, one of the first women to hold a senior position at Seagram, told Tony, who was her supervisor at the time, that she was planning on resigning from the company. He couldn't believe it because she was such an important contributor to the company in terms of planning and budgeting. One of her children was having a learning issue. Judy decided that her son was more important than her job and that the best way to help him avoid falling behind in school was for her to be home for him before and after school so she could help him stay on top of his schoolwork. Tony didn't want to lose her—and he knew I didn't, either—so he suggested she work part-time in the middle of the day, while her son was at school.

Today, this sounds like a perfectly logical way to handle this situation, but back in the 1980s and '90s, part-time executives were unheard of. Even so, after Tony and Judy worked out a plan, Tony came to me and asked for my okay. Later, he told me he thought there was a pretty good chance that "Old-School Ed" would not approve it, but saying no didn't even enter my mind. Of course Judy should put her family first. And of course we didn't want to lose her. So we gave her a part-time position, and everything worked out perfectly. Her son caught up in school, and when the situation changed, she returned to work full-time and remained a valued member of our team. Later, when parts of Seagram were acquired by Pernod Ricard, Judy was Seagram's key representative in the acquisition. In doing the right thing for Judy, we also did the right thing for Seagram.

• • •

My final story about doing the right thing is also one of my favorite anecdotes from a career filled with many memorable moments. In 1994, when I was president and CEO of the Spirits and Wine Group at Seagram, we identified the need to add a strong vodka brand to the Seagram family. Sales of "brown" spirits such as whiskey, bourbon, rum, and cognac were softening in part because young people were developing a preference for "white" spirits such as vodka, tequila, and gin. (An adage in the spirits industry is that young people don't want to drink the same kinds of alcoholic beverages as their parents.) We set our sights on creating a partnership with Stolichnaya, the Russian company that at the time produced one of the world's top vodka brands.

After some behind-the-scenes negotiating with the Russian government, which owned Stoli, I headed to Moscow with some of my team to try to get the ball rolling on a deal. When we arrived, we met with a top Russian official and about twenty of his assistants. The official listened carefully to us as we explained our interest in the brand, and he seemed engaged. But then he explained what it would take for us to make an agreement. Before we could discuss any details of a potential deal, he said, Seagram would have to deposit $100 million into his personal account in an offshore bank.

To say that I was stunned wouldn't even begin to describe what I felt when he made this demand. This man—this top government official—demanded a $100 million bribe that we would have to pay to him personally before we could even start the negotiation process with his government. And he made this demand in front of a room full of other Russian officials. He wasn't even trying to hide it.

That was how the Russian government worked at the time. But it wasn't how I worked.

I told the government official that his proposal sounded interesting but I would have to discuss it with Edgar Bronfman Sr., chairman and CEO of Seagram. However, knowing that getting Stoli would require Seagram to deal with such openly corrupt people, I had no intention of bringing this deal to Edgar or taking the negotiations with the Russians any further. There was no way I would play any part in giving this guy a $100 million bribe—not only because it was such a case of blatant dishonesty, but because I had no doubt it would likely be the first of many bribes we would be asked to pay and the beginning of an unending stream of dishonesty we would have to endure.

Instead, we got on a plane and flew to Sweden to talk to the people who called the shots at Absolut Vodka. Like Stolichnaya, Absolut was owned by its government. But unlike the Russians, the Swedes had no expectation of receiving bribes. In Sweden, we met with a small group of government officials charged with running Absolut. I told them I'd like to negotiate an arrangement for Seagram to acquire long-term worldwide distribution rights for Absolut. They thought it was an excellent idea, and before I knew it, I had a deal with the Swedes, people who couldn't have been nicer, more businesslike, or honest. Within three months, Seagram took control of Absolut worldwide. And every step of the way, we had a fabulous working relationship with our Swedish counterparts. They had a moral code that could not have been any higher.

What made the Absolut deal even sweeter was that we stole this prize product from our number one competitor, Diageo, which was then United Distillers. Seagram and United Distillers were like the Yankees and the Red

Sox—fierce competitors who loved to beat the other team. We convinced the Swedes that we would treat Absolut like a champion and build it into a top international brand, which was exactly what we did. It was a major industry coup and one of my proudest moments at Seagram. To this day, I've held on to a congratulatory note about the Absolut contract that I received from Charles R. Bronfman, Edgar Bronfman Sr.'s brother. The deal "speaks volumes about the kind of organization you have built over the years," Charles wrote. "Today is a really good day for Seagram. You deserve all the plaudits that will come your way. Well, well done."

After we completed the deal, I really wanted to do something to thank the Swedes for working with us in such an honest way. So I asked if there was anything I could offer them in the way of a gift that they would feel comfortable accepting. They had mentioned that they enjoyed fly-fishing, so I offered to take them on a fly-fishing trip. After seeking and receiving authorization from the Swedish government, they said it was within the scope of their ethics guidelines to accept a brief fly-fishing excursion. I found out that the best fly-fishing in the world was in Iceland, and I arranged to take them there for a few days as a way to celebrate our deal and thank them for their business.

I had never been fly-fishing before, but I enjoy other outdoor activities like skiing and tennis, so I was game to give it a try. I flew to a remote part of Iceland, checked in to the best fishing resort in the country, put on angling waders, and stepped into what could have been the coldest river on the face of the earth. The Swedes were enjoying themselves immensely, but I realized after about fifteen minutes that there was no way in hell I could spend five days standing in that water. So I "accidentally" fell over and got soaked. "You keep fishing," I told the Swedes. "I'll head back to the cabin to change." I ended up spending the remainder of the week on dry land, watching them fish. They had the time of their lives, and I had the satisfaction of knowing that these honest, ethical government officials were enjoying themselves.

• • •

Doing the right thing doesn't always pay off immediately or obviously. But in my experience, it usually comes back to you in some way. As I mentioned earlier, I attended my friend Fernando Kfouri's eightieth birthday party in New York a couple of years ago. So many of the people I had hired or promoted over the years were there. Although it was Fernando's birthday, I received a wonderful gift during the festivities: an understanding of the impact I had had on the lives of some of the people I worked with. It really was mind-blowing. Forgive me if it sounds like I'm tooting my own horn here, but at my age, I claim the right to indulge in a little of this kind of reflection. It really wasn't until the night of Fernando's party, when one person after another thanked me for giving them some of the biggest lucky breaks of their lives, that I realized how much my actions had affected so many of the people I've worked with over the years.

I had never thought that by giving people opportunities to progress and to have access to advancement in international positions, I was doing anything other than treating them the way I would want to be treated myself. But in hindsight, I can appreciate in a way that I couldn't in real time that a fair number of people had better, more successful, more exciting lives because of opportunities I was lucky enough to be able to give them. They had prepared themselves to be lucky, and I realize now that I was in the wonderful position to be able to provide them with the luck for which they had prepared. To this day, I feel overwhelmingly thankful to George Bremser at General Foods for giving me one of the biggest lucky breaks of my life. But it wasn't until the night of Fernando's party that I realized that the whole thing had come full circle. Not only had I been on the receiving end of quite a few lucky breaks, but I was happy to realize that I'd doled some out, too.

And now I'm going to try to keep this circle of respect and opportunity going by asking you to do two things. First, always treat people with respect. And second, whenever you have a chance to give someone a lucky break, do it. If they're prepared for it, they'll flourish. And you will have had a chance not only to do the right thing but to have an amazing impact on them. Believe me when I tell you that it will stand out as a highlight of your life. It's a win-win situation for everyone.

A GOOD MAN

You never know what your children notice when they're growing up—what stories they pick up on, what memories they hold on to. The following story takes place in Kibon when my son Ted was around ten or eleven years old. I had no idea he was aware that this had happened, but it obviously made an impression on him. I look back at this story with great pride, and I'm pleased to see that Ted does also. Here's the story from Ted's view.

One day I asked Mario, who worked as our driver in São Paulo, an innocent childhood question. The question might have come from a school lesson or something I read in fourth-grade Bible class.

"When do you know someone is a good person, Mario? And is my dad a good person?"

Mario's immediate response surprised me: "Your dad is a very good man, Ted."

But I wanted to be convinced, so I asked him, "How do you know?"

Mario told me he had a story that he wanted me to keep secret. I agreed, and I didn't talk about it for over forty years. Until now.

Mario told me a story about a friendship between a newspaper vendor and the president of a large ice cream company in Brazil.

"Every day, your father would stop the car for a few minutes at the factory gates, get out of the car, and buy a newspaper from this man," Mario said. "Your father did not need to stop and buy a newspaper, as it could be delivered to his office, but this was his daily ritual. A relationship began between these two men. They became familiar with each other's families, their interests, and their business. They enjoyed chatting and joking and laughing together."

These visits at the newsstand continued, day after day, year after year. But then, one day, the man at the newsstand was not there. And he wasn't there for several days after. "Your father asked me where the man was, but I didn't know," Mario told me. "I checked around and found out the man was unwell. He had a potentially fatal form of cancer."

Mario told my father how sick the newspaper vendor was. When my father asked what the man was doing to get better, Mario told him that the man's religion would not allow him to use medication or have an operation. He could only seek healing through prayer. "And even if he wanted an operation, he would most likely be unable to pay for it," Mario explained.

My father asked Mario to find out where the man lived. Once the address was located, my father told Mario to take him there.

Mario tried to talk my father out of this visit, because the news vendor lived in an unsafe *favela*, a poor, run-down area that was extremely dangerous. But my father would not be talked out of the visit.

"Your father and I got out of the car and walked up to the front door of the home," Mario told me. "When the door opened, the family was shocked to see 'Mr. Kibon' standing there." They invited my father and Mario in and sat down with them at their kitchen table.

"Your dad began to speak about the newspaper vendor's relationship with his young children and his wife and how hard it would be for them if he died," Mario explained. "He asked the man about his cancer and the effects it had and found out it was causing problems with the man's leg. He also listened to the man explain the rules his religion had against medicine and operations."

My father heard the man out and then shared some stories about his own life and the importance of him being there for his own wife and children. Dad stressed how much the man's family needed him.

Lengthy discussions followed, and eventually, a change of heart occurred. My father and the newspaper vendor agreed to work together to find a treatment for his cancer.

"Your father paid for his operation and supported his family until he was back to work," Mario said. "The man had to have his leg amputated, but he survived."

After hearing that story, I realized Mario was right: my father was a truly good person. And the next day, when I went with Mario to pick up my dad from work, he pointed out the one-legged man standing next to the newsstand and said, "That is your father's friend."

4

THINK BIG

I STAYED AT KIBON FOR ABOUT EIGHT YEARS. During that time, my executive team and I, in collaboration with Kibon workers, had turned the company around and set it firmly on solid financial ground. When I left, it was the third largest international profit contributor within General Foods.

I absolutely loved living in Brazil, but it was time to move on. From a professional standpoint, I was ready for new challenges. Big challenges. So I decided I would go after the franchise rights to bottle and sell Pepsi in Brazil. This necessitated an enormous amount of legwork, negotiating, and maneuvering—and it required me to take some big risks. But the rewards would be enormous, so I felt it was worth the effort to do all that groundwork. My plan was to win the bottling and distribution franchise in Brazil and then expand it to other South American countries. Coca-Cola was the number one soft drink in Brazil at the time, and I saw an enormous opportunity for Pepsi to challenge and overtake the market leader.

Unfortunately, just when I thought the franchise deal would land in my hands, it was given to someone else. I knew this might happen, but still, I was surprised when it did. As someone who believes in doing the right thing, I tend to assume others will, too. But not this time. The Pepsi franchise went to someone who had connections in high places, and that was it for my plan to become the Pepsi franchise king of South America.

Disappointments are a normal part of business, especially when you're dealing with international players. The price you pay for thinking big is occasionally losing big. That's okay—it comes with the territory— and it certainly wasn't the last time I failed to get something I was going after. So after the Pepsi deal fell through, I picked myself up, dusted myself off, and looked around for another opportunity.

What I really would have liked was to be named head of international business for all of General Foods. However, international business had grown to become a much larger part of General Foods than it had been when I was sent to Kibon. I believed in thinking big, and I felt quite confident that I could handle a top international position at General Foods, but I also knew there was no way the company would move me into such a high-level position at that point because there were too many experienced, well-connected executives already waiting in line for the top international job. So I started looking around for other opportunities that would position me for a high-level job at a major international organization.

That's when Pillsbury came knocking. It was 1974, and Pillsbury, which had started as a flour mill in Minneapolis, Minnesota, more than a hundred years earlier, had grown into one of the world's largest food companies. After my successful run at Kibon, I was a perfect fit to take a top leadership role in Pillsbury's international business, starting with Latin America. Pillsbury was in the midst of an expansion that included the acquisition of various other food-related companies; it was even buying up some restaurants, including the Burger King chain. The Pillsbury consumer products group, which was just one of several divisions within the company, produced and distributed a wide range of grocery products, including baked goods, frozen and canned vegetables, and cake mixes, to name just a few.

When I joined Pillsbury, it was poised to significantly grow its international business with expansion into various countries. I was charged with, among many other tasks, selling or turning around underperforming business units and acquiring, building up, or expanding units that could increase the company's worldwide presence. I expanded and bought companies throughout Europe, particularly in the United Kingdom, Germany, and France. And we negotiated manufacturing arrangements with various European companies to use their production facilities to produce Pillsbury foods in Europe when it didn't make sense for Pillsbury to build and operate its own production plants.

By the time I left Pillsbury in 1981 as the company's international group president, we had tripled its international profits. So overall it was a win, but my time with the company started off with some bumps. When I was first hired by Pillsbury, my family and I moved from São Paulo to Wayzata, Minnesota, a suburb of Minneapolis located on the shores of Lake Minnetonka. It was a beautiful town where many of the rich people in Minnesota lived. I figured I'd fit in pretty well because I generally had no problem making new friends. But I soon discovered that the Minneapolis area was not interested in opening up its arms to Ed McDonnell and his family. I expected neighbors and coworkers to reach out to us, but it didn't happen. Nobody in the neighborhood invited us over or even talked to us when we moved in. And when I tried to join the country club, I was told to wait ten years to make an application. Then, ten years after that, I might be accepted. So I built a tennis court and swimming pool at my home instead.

I wondered at first if our neighbors didn't like Irish people, but I don't think that was the problem. The fact that we were Catholic probably didn't help our case because these people were all very WASPy. Rather, they considered us outsiders, and none of them had an interest in socializing with people they hadn't known their whole lives. It was a very close-knit society where everyone was a member of a wealthy family that owned a business in town. They just didn't have a need to be friendly because they already had the friends with whom they'd grown up and gone to school.

Three months after moving in, I invited everyone in the neighborhood to my house for a huge cocktail party. I spared no expense and made sure it was one of the best parties ever. People were happy to attend, had a great time, and raved afterward that it was the best party they'd been to in a long time. I was thrilled. I figured they'd soon reciprocate with invitations to their own parties and our social isolation would come to an end. But none came. Everyone just disappeared back into their own circles.

This was hard for me because I'm a very social person. It was hard on my wife and my three children also. We were all ignored, and what's more, my children disliked their schools. It was ironic: one of the reasons Kay and I decided we should move back to the United States was so our children could have some exposure to American culture. All of our children had been born in the United States, but we moved to Brazil when they were small, and they had spent far more time in Brazil than in the States. And although we had recently bought a house in Hilton Head, South Carolina, to serve as a home base of sorts in the US, our children really didn't know America very well. Oddly, in moving to Minnesota, we all felt far more isolated than we had in Brazil.

I had never before lived in Middle America, nor did I know anything about Middle America before I took the job at Pillsbury and moved to Minnesota. But I soon figured out that Middle America was the wrong place for me and my family. On top of the insular social atmosphere, the weather in Minnesota was horrendous and uninviting. After the tropical summers and balmy winters in São Paulo, my family and I really struggled to endure frigid Wayzata winters. It was awful.

Fortunately, our time in Minnesota was short. It soon made more sense for us to be living in London, and we all felt thrilled to make the move. My children quickly settled in at the American School in London, where they had much more in common with their ex-patriot classmates than with the closed-off kids in Minnesota. And my wife, who, like me, was an avid tennis player and golfer, was much happier in London, where we spent many happy hours near our home, playing tennis in Regent's Park. We lived very well in London, with chauffeurs and friendly neighbors and a vibrant social life. Our life there was in every way the opposite of our life in Minnesota, and we appreciated it all the more because of our time in that cold, closed-off community.

Once we got away from Minnesota and were settled in London, we were happy with Pillsbury, and I enjoyed my work there. The Pillsbury employees who worked overseas were much friendlier than those who were marooned in Minneapolis. It was a very busy time—a very successful time. By acquiring new companies and pushing into various European countries, we helped make Pillsbury a truly international company.

After several years working with Pillsbury in London, I was asked to transfer back to Minnesota to work in our headquarters. I could absolutely not picture going back—there was no way in hell I was going to move back permanently from London to Minneapolis. I started looking around for another opportunity and soon found one.

Unfortunately, the unpleasantness continued when I announced that I was leaving the company. The chairman of Pillsbury told me he was furious that I was quitting, and he threatened to destroy me if I carried through with my plans to resign. He said that if I left, he would make accusations against me that would sabotage my career. His vindictiveness was very unpleasant—he accused me of cheating on my expense accounts, among other things. Very nasty. But I was never dishonest, and I had nothing to hide. Nonetheless, his actions infuriated me. I told him to his face that for every false statement he made about me, I would hire away two Pillsbury employees and take them with me to my next job. And sure enough, when people heard that I was leaving, many of them volunteered immediately to come with me. We all wanted to get away from Pillsbury.

The Pillsbury years were a bit of a mixed bag for me, but I always felt that I came out ahead because of the experiences I had, the people I met, the successes I achieved, and the fact that my time at Pillsbury helped prepare me for the best job of my career: running the international business at Seagram.

● ● ●

When I decided I was finished with Pillsbury, I began to look around for other opportunities. Once again, I was thinking big. Really big. Although I was desperate to avoid spending any more time in frosty Minneapolis, I wasn't about to accept a lateral move just to get out of an unfriendly city. I knew what I wanted: to run the international business in one of the world's largest corporations. I had the experience and the record of success; I was ready for the big time.

I found what I was looking for with the Seagram Company.

Seagram had a long, storied history, with roots going back to a distillery started in Montreal in 1857 by a Canadian named Joseph E. Seagram. After various transformations, this business eventually ended up in the hands of Samuel Bronfman, a Jewish refugee who had migrated with his wealthy family from Russia to Canada in 1889. Bronfman had founded a company called the Distillers Corporation in 1924 and got rich during Prohibition selling liquor to bootleggers who served the thirsty US market, especially in the Chicago area. (Bronfman had control over alcohol shipments from Canada to the Midwest; the East Coast belonged to a group that included Joseph P. Kennedy Sr., and a couple of other groups had purview over the West Coast.) When Bronfman acquired the company that had come to be known as Joseph E. Seagram & Sons in 1928, he merged it with his Distillers Corporation and renamed the combined business the Seagram Company.

Certainly, Samuel Bronfman thought big. He produced and stockpiled millions of cases of Canadian whisky during US Prohibition, and when liquor sales in the United States became legal again, he flooded the market with his huge inventory of liquor, which made the Bronfman family very, very wealthy.

Over the years, Bronfman grew Seagram by buying various distilleries and vintners around the world, including Captain Morgan, Myers's, and Chivas Regal. In the 1950s, he began investing in oil and coal companies, and by 1965, the company had total sales exceeding $1 billion.

Samuel's son Edgar had started working at Seagram in 1950, when he was twenty-one; eventually, his father put him in charge of the company's US operations, while placing his brother Charles at the head of the House of Seagram in Canada. When Samuel died in 1971, Edgar took over for his father as chairman and CEO, and in 1977, Seagram sales reached $2.2 billion. Edgar continued to build Seagram's liquor business and added a big cash generator to its portfolio when it acquired 25 percent of the shares of the petrochemical company DuPont in 1981. Seagram's brands included VO Canadian, Crown Royal, Chivas Regal, Glenlivet, Martell Cognac, Mumm Champagne, and many others.

Although Seagram was by all accounts a successful company when I joined in 1981, its liquor sales had softened. Drinking habits in the United States were changing, and Seagram sales were falling as people began to lose interest in the blended whiskies for which Seagram was known. By 1981, Edgar was between a rock and a hard place; he felt intense pressure to increase Seagram's liquor sales, but he wasn't sure how to squeeze more out of the North American market. Seagram had been in his family for generations, and as the eldest son of Samuel Bronfman, he felt the expectation of success weighing heavily on his shoulders. But how could he grow the company when the North American market, which supplied the lion's share of its profits, seemed saturated?

That's where I came in.

It was time for Seagram to think big—really big—and start looking beyond the United States and Canada to grow its business. At the time, only about one-fifth of Seagram's sales (about $1 billion) came from outside North America. Seagram had a unique opportunity to roar into the international market and expand its business throughout the world. In fact, as Edgar Bronfman Sr. and I discussed during my first meeting with him, one of Seagram's best chances—perhaps its only chance—for future success in its core liquor business was to tap into the growing global market and expand itself overseas.

I believed in Seagram's potential to become an international success story. And I also believed I was the person who could bring about that success. I was thinking bigger than I had at any other time in my career.

Fortunately, Edgar Bronfman Sr. agreed with me.

And so in 1981, at the age of forty-five, I was hired by the Seagram Company to be president of Seagram International. I would move to New York and take responsibility for all Seagram business outside the United States and Canada.

It was the job for which I had been preparing myself my entire career.

A WORLD OF POSSIBILITIES

My son Paul is not only my business partner; he's also my friend. I asked him to contribute some thoughts about his upbringing, and here's what he had to say:

When I was growing up, my father always encouraged my brother and sister and me to think big. We knew he was a self-made guy who came from a poor family, and we knew that he had worked his way up. Thanks to hard work and a lot of luck, he had become extremely successful in his business career—but he never pushed us to do anything other than to work diligently in school. And he always made it clear that he wanted us to think big and that he and my mother would support us in whatever we decided to do.

We grew up differently than most other kids. We lived in Brazil when we were young. That just seemed like the normal way of life, but we realized when we came back to the United States to visit our cousins and later to move to Minnesota that not everybody lived like we did. To us, it was strange that our cousins lived in the same house all their life and didn't speak Portuguese. We didn't realize it was strange that our four-year-old sister would translate from Portuguese to English for our mother in the Brazilian grocery store. Even so, we did have the sense that we were living a special kind of existence and that my father had done something extraordinary with his life. I think we all felt free to pursue our own dreams.

A lot of our summers were spent working at different distilleries. When all my friends were going to Cape Cod or places like that for summer jobs, I'd be working at one of the Seagram chateaus in France. In hindsight, they were great opportunities, and although of course I didn't realize it at the time, they helped prepare me for my future.

After graduating from Boston University, I moved to Los Angeles to become an actor. I had a passion for musical theater, and looking back, I realize I had learned a lot about acting during childhood and adolescence, always being the new kid in school, always having to figure out very quickly how to deal with people and fit in to new situations. When I finished college, I thought, "I'm going to go straight out to Hollywood and become a star." I did some walk-on work and a lot of extra work, but I ended up waiting tables more than anything else. I eventually realized acting wasn't for me, but it meant a lot to me that my parents supported me while I explored it.

I ended up getting into the entertainment business by doing public relations for television and celebrity clients, both in Los Angeles and New York. Then I started working with Ed after he left Seagram and started a liquor distribution business in the Philippines and US Virgin Islands. (I always called him Ed at work because it's not a good look to call the boss "Dad" in meetings.) All three of us were given the opportunity to enroll in a Seagram training program after college. My brother, Ted, was the only one who took it on—I had no desire to do that back then. But it's funny: we all ended up working for my dad in the liquor business at one point or another, although in different countries and in different capacities.

Both of my parents were incredibly supportive of me when I

told them I was gay. I was in my twenties, living in Los Angeles, and it was the height of the AIDS crisis when I came out. I had been living a double life, keeping my sexuality a secret from my family—or so I thought. When I came out to my father, he said, "Why didn't you tell me sooner? We've all known for years that you are gay."

And I said, "If you knew, why didn't you ask me about it?"

And he said, "Because your mother wouldn't let me. But do you know how many times I took you out drinking in hopes that you'd open up?" That's the cool thing about Ed. Even though he came from a background where that probably wouldn't have been accepted, he was always incredibly open-minded. I had friends who were dying of AIDS, and when they came out, their families cut them off and refused to let them come home. But I was one of the fortunate ones who had his family's support while trying to navigate through a world that wasn't always so kind to gay men.

I have always felt that Ed was proud of me. He was living a life that was so much more than anything he had ever dreamed of, but he never put pressure on me to be like him or to do what he had done. He accepted me as I was and am. To this day, he's thrilled just to hear that one of us is doing something interesting. I think he just wants us to be happy.

5

DEVELOP LASTING BUSINESS RELATIONSHIPS

June 25, 1991

Dear Ed,

I know this is not the exact date, but nevertheless you and we are celebrating 10 years that you have been with Seagram.

I not only congratulate you, I congratulate us. You, and thus we, have gone from strength to strength. Your numbers, and thus our numbers, speak for themselves. The fact that you have recently been asked to accept the challenge of running our Spirits and Wine business worldwide speaks for itself, too.

On a personal note, you are fun to work with. Your great success is probably due to the fact that you are also fun to work for (although I can't personally attest to that, but there are many who can).

Like any successful marriage, we have been good for each other. You have really understood Seagram and what it means, and more, you have expanded that meaning with your sincerity, hard work, and devotion to all who are involved with you.

God bless,

Edgar

I've had many wonderful relationships with business colleagues over the years, but one of the best was my friendship with Edgar Bronfman Sr., who hired me at Seagram. It wasn't always an easy relationship, and it certainly had its share of challenges and difficult moments. But through it all—Seagram's spectacular success and then its spectacular failure—Edgar and I remained friends. Good friends. He sometimes referred to our relationship as a marriage of sorts, and that was an apt description in that we stayed connected to each other for better and for worse, for richer and for poorer, and in sickness and in health, until Edgar's death at the age of eighty-four.

Edgar Bronfman Sr. was a fascinating person with a background that could not have been more different from mine. He was born in 1929, just a couple of months before the US stock market collapsed and threw the country into the Great Depression. Edgar grew up wealthy in the shadow of his father, Samuel Bronfman, a tyrannical man who founded the company that eventually became Seagram. Edgar had a difficult relationship with his father. He told me that his father never once told him that he loved him, nor did Samuel ever give Edgar credit for any of the things he did at Seagram. Edgar described his childhood as being "mostly unhappy" because of his remote, inaccessible mother and his driven, insecure, egotistical father. "My childhood was marked by a tension between privilege on the one hand and emotional dysfunction on the other," Edgar wrote in his 1998 book, *Good Spirits: The Making of a Businessman.*

From the very beginning, Edgar had held the position of Seagram heir apparent. "My father was an empire builder. And, true to the customs of his time, the emperor needed a male heir. As the first son among four children born to my parents, I was destined to be that heir." But rather than feeling a closer attachment to his father because of his status as the chosen one, Edgar felt restricted by it. "In truth, Sam Bronfman wanted a clone. That fact goes a long way toward explaining why my childhood was more of an endurance test than a time of nurture. Father's dreams of passing on his empire were eventually realized, but at a cost."

Intellectually, Edgar was a brilliant man. As a businessman, he was a visionary, a creative thinker, and a tough but supportive leader. Edgar never pretended to be a line manager, however, and he left the day-to-day running of the businesses to people like me. He gave me the space to do what I was good at, and it paid off. During my time working for him, we expanded the Seagram Spirits and Wine business into over fifty countries via acquisitions and/or start-ups. We also spearheaded the purchase of Tropicana, the orange juice company, and other major players.

In addition to his work at Seagram, Edgar served as president of the World Jewish Congress, an international federation of Jewish communities first established in 1936 in response to the wave of anti-Semitism spreading across Europe. Under Edgar's leadership from 1979 to 2007, the World Jewish Congress took a number of history-making actions, such as exposing the Nazi past of former United Nations secretary-general Kurt Waldheim and pressuring for the restitution of assets of Holocaust victims held in bank accounts in Switzerland and elsewhere to their rightful owners. Edgar received both admiration and criticism for the group's tactics during his time as president.

If you had to describe Edgar in one word, it would be "elegant." Tall and extremely handsome, he turned heads when he walked into a room. He was a real lady's man. A playboy. But that didn't interfere with our

friendship. Edgar married five times. His first wife, Ann Loeb, a bank-
ing heiress, was the only wealthy woman he ever married. They had five
children, including Samuel II—who in the 1970s was kidnapped, held for
ransom, and safely returned—and Edgar Jr., who would play a big role in
my life. Then he married Lady Carolyn Townshend of the British royal
family, but that marriage lasted a very short time, perhaps only ten days.
Next, he married Rita Webb, known as "Georgiana," whom he divorced
and remarried and divorced a second time. His last wife was Jan Aronson,
with whom he stayed until his death.

I first met Edgar Bronfman Sr. at my Seagram job interview in 1981.
I had heard about the position through a headhunting group that I had
contacted when I was looking for a way to get out of Pillsbury. Right
around the time I called the headhunters, Edgar reached out to them to
find someone to head up the new international division that Seagram was
forming. I met with Edgar after several screening meetings with various
other people. By that point, my hiring was a foregone conclusion; the
goal of our conversation was to get Edgar's seal of approval to hire me as
president of Seagram International.

Considering how important this step was for Seagram and for me,
Edgar and I had a remarkably short meeting—probably about fifteen or
twenty minutes. We chatted about the company and some of my ideas
about expanding Seagram into global markets. And then, before I knew
it, the interview had ended. We stood up, Edgar shook my hand, and he
offered me the job. Then he said something that surprised me:

"Ed, I guarantee you, if you do well by me, you will be comfortable
for the rest of your life."

I certainly liked the sound of that. "It's a deal," I said. And thus began
my sixteen-year career at Seagram. When I was hired, I was based in
New York—I bought an apartment at 30 Sutton Place in Manhattan—

but throughout my career at Seagram, I split my time between New York and London.

During those years, Edgar and I both kept up our end of that bargain. I did well by him, and he made sure I was comfortable for the rest of my life. But neither of us had any way of knowing at that moment how high our highs and how low our lows would be.

I later learned that one of the things about me that appealed to Edgar was that he knew, based on my reputation, that I would never lie to him. He was an honorable man, and he expected honesty from others. Unfortunately, honor was sometimes in short supply in the people working at the company. Before I came along, Edgar was surrounded by too many people who were more inclined to tell him what he *wanted* to hear rather than what he *needed* to hear. I think that by hiring me, he was attempting to change that. Edgar also knew that I had been successful in every job I'd held before Seagram. And I made it clear during the vetting process that I was very enthusiastic about the job. Holding a position like this—being president of Seagram International—was exactly what I had been working toward. My big opportunity. Once again, I had received a very lucky break—but a break for which I had long been preparing.

And of course, it made perfect sense to have an Irish Catholic from Boston running a drinks company.

BREAKING THE MOLD

My friend Tony Rodriguez, who worked with me at Seagram and rose to the level of executive vice president and deputy CEO, has a memory like a steel trap. I asked him to share some recollections of what Seagram was like back in the early 1980s, when we both launched our careers there. Here's what he has to say.

Ed and I both started at Seagram at around the same time. Ed's hiring represented a fundamental cultural change within the organization. The talent bench at Seagram had been overly concentrated from within the company, and this was the first time they'd gone outside the company for a top hire. But it wasn't the last time—it was a practice that Ed would continue during his years at Seagram.

Ed's hiring at Seagram was groundbreaking in another way also: although he had international brand success and experience marketing for a global consumer products company, he was an accountant, not a marketer, by training and education. In those days, finance people and accounting people were seen as being more limited and were rarely hired for top management jobs. But thanks to Ed and a few other people who came out of the finance and accounting side, they eventually became known as the folks who understood the economics of the business and, if they were the right kind of broad-minded executives, could be general management potential with the finance and economics as an underpinning.

Seagram reached out to Ed because at that time, culturally and financially, it was a domestic company. Pure and simple. It had grown out of the bootlegging era with the Bronfman family and their post-Prohibition network of Jewish distributors. And that's the only world they knew. But then Edgar Bronfman Sr. brings in this blond, bright-eyed Irish-Catholic guy from Boston. It wasn't too threatening at first because Ed was hired to start an international operation, and very few people at Seagram had confidence that an international group would do well because we had so many internationally established competitors. The US guys at Seagram thought the rest of the world wasn't worth the effort.

Ed not only had substantial international experience, he also quickly started bringing in some very talented people he'd worked with elsewhere—people like Myron Roeder from Pillsbury and Fernando Kfouri from Kibon and General Foods. They were a class act. I was in my midtwenties at the time, and I just remember that they were a different breed, the three of them in particular, compared to the rough-and-tumble New York sales guys, which was the culture at Seagram.

People really didn't expect much from Ed. But he came in with his immense people skills, which took them by surprise. He led people to underrate him on purpose. I was in many meetings with him, and I soon knew him well enough to see what he was doing: he would underplay his cards as a way of giving other people an opening to overplay their cards, and then *bam*. Boy, would he surprise them.

Ed had world-class leadership skills. I use him as an example when I mentor young alumni and professionals who often judge people by where they went to school. Ed went to Suffolk University, but he was a better leader than most Harvard MBAs. He was just such a natural when it came to management and strategic planning.

When Ed assembled his team at Seagram, he told us we had to be ready to fight for resources. That was part of growing the international business and reducing Seagram's corporate dependency on the US market. Sometimes the corporate powers that be were biased against our small international group because the company had been so dominated by the US market. When we went into places like Korea and Latin America, we were going in with one hand tied behind our backs because the people who controlled the Seagram purse strings had ethnic and cultural biases, and they saw the United States as being the better source of return on investment, even though it often wasn't. So we had to make twice as good a case in order to get the investment funds we needed and get management behind us.

But Ed knew what he was doing. We never had any doubt about that.

My first day on the job at Seagram, Edgar invited me to a charitable event for the World Jewish Congress. One of the top guys in the liquor business came over to me and said, "Ed McDonnell, what the hell is an Irishman doing running this company?" It made me laugh like hell.

One of the people I met at that event was Marty Bart, who was one of Seagram's top executives at the time. I'll let Marty tell that story:

There were about a thousand people at that event. Ed walked in and knew absolutely no one in the entire place. I saw him and I felt bad because he was all by himself. So I walked up to him and introduced myself and said, "Ed, I hope you don't think I'm overdoing it, but why don't you come sit with us?" He loved it! He sat right down, and we all got along great. And it was hysterical, because we all had to give donations to this Jewish organization, which he didn't realize. I don't think he even knew who was sponsoring the event. But we had a great time. Our friendship took off from there, and we've been friends ever since.

Even though being Jewish was important to Edgar, he had no problem with the fact that I came from an Irish-Catholic upbringing. Perhaps because he had experienced bias, he did not want to engage in bias. Not that we didn't joke around about our respective backgrounds. One story still makes me laugh to this day. I lived in London for much of the time I worked for Seagram because that's where the action was. Edgar and I were both members of a private club called Harry's Bar. One day Princess Diana was there having lunch with another woman, and Edgar couldn't take his eyes off her. Neither could I, to be honest—she had the most stunning legs I'd ever seen. When she got up to leave, we noticed that she curtsied to a gentleman who was sitting at the table next to us. "What the hell is she curtsying to that guy for?" Edgar asked me.

"Probably because that's King Hussein of Jordan," I said.

"Well, that pisses me off," Edgar said. "He's the king of the Arabs. Doesn't she realize I'm the king of the Jews?"

One of my priorities at Seagram was to start cleaning house. Edgar had some people working for him in the ranks of top management who were simply not qualified for their jobs—lots of hangers-on who wanted to stay comfortable rather than pushing the company to grow. When he hired me, he had been running Seagram for about ten years, and I think he was realizing that surrounding himself with yes-men wasn't helping him or the company. Of course, he did have some second thoughts once I started getting rid of these people, but luckily, he had a close friend keeping an eye on me whom he trusted and with whom I could speak frankly, and this guy understood exactly what I was doing and why I was doing it. Between the two of us, we managed to keep Edgar invested in the need for a shake-up. We both knew there were too many top executives who were more interested in doing what was good for themselves than for the company. Edgar wanted Seagram to flourish, and he was beginning to realize that he needed to go outside the company to find the people who could make that happen. Hiring me and some other executives turned out to be key to Seagram's future success, and it never would have happened if Edgar hadn't had the courage and the common sense to allow me to go shake the company up a bit.

Seagram was in a state of chaos when I started working there. Consumption of distilled spirits in the United States was falling, and alcohol taxes were rising. The company had lost some of its earning power, and I had my work cut out for me. But I knew exactly what I needed to do. First, I had to hire a team of good people—including some people I had worked with at General Foods and Pillsbury. Next, I had to fix the company's base business by divesting or closing down nonviable businesses and brands and turning around viable but money-losing international businesses. I also focused on new business development by acquiring and integrating fifteen companies and negotiating and establishing five joint venture companies with local partners in countries around the globe. By the time I retired from Seagram in 1995, all forty-five of its affiliated companies worldwide were profitable, an achievement of which I am quite proud.

In the liquor business, then as now, marketing of brands is the key to success. Chivas Regal was Seagram's number one Scotch whisky brand. Although it was well known, it wasn't living up to its potential, so I focused on marketing it around the world. China was just opening up at the time, and by investing in marketing, my team and I made it the most successful Scotch whisky brand in Asia and eventually the world. But that took focus and lots of marketing money.

At the beginning, I was hired strictly to grow the international part of the business. So I just focused on key brands that had the potential to be world class, such as Chivas Regal. I concentrated most of my efforts on identifying and entering new markets, investing in marketing, and making sure our pricing was in line with what the markets could handle. I hired top people for each of the countries I was trying to open up for Seagram, and we invested in very aggressive marketing.

Once our marketing efforts started to take hold, growth began to sky-rocket. The domestic side of the company couldn't believe the growth we were accomplishing in the international group. We made big inroads in various countries, especially China, Thailand, Japan, and Australia. Australia in particular was a very good liquor market, but Seagram was unknown up until that point because the company had never made any kind of big marketing effort there before. Once we did, sales started to explode.

Seagram International's success shocked everyone. I had always believed that there was plenty of room for growth in international markets. Other US liquor companies had had success expanding globally, and my attitude was that Seagram could too. But none of us realized that Seagram could capture those markets as successfully as it did.

Credit for some of our success must go to James Espey, a marketing genius I hired away from United Distillers, where he was building the Johnnie Walker brand in the Asia-Pacific region. James and I ran into each other a few times, and we got along well. While having a drink together one evening, I told him, "You enjoy having a decent whisky with me, and you don't really like working for the other guy. Let me know when the time comes for you to switch." Sure enough that time came, and when it did, I hired him and gave him the job of running and building Chivas Brothers globally.

I knew James was a big thinker. But even so, I nearly fell over when he asked us to approve a long-term Chivas Regal marketing and development plan with a budget of $100 million. That was a hell of a lot of money. Here's what James says about that today:

Chivas Regal was the biggest brand in the entire Seagram portfolio, and I wanted $100 million because we needed to start distilling more at that point so we would have enough stock for many years in the future—twenty years or even more. We had to be sure we had enough good whisky stock available to meet the demand we intended to generate. The liquor industry is a long-term industry, and you have to think ahead. Far ahead. When whisky is distilled, it is put in wood and it stays in barrels for ten, fifteen, twenty years or more, depending on what you want to do with it. The real value comes much later. I got Ed's support, and we invested $90 million in distillation and forward stock so we'd have plenty for the future. We also spent $10 million on buying and furnishing a hospitality home (Linn House) for Chivas Brothers and to upgrade distilleries to make them attractive for tourism. Every tourist who enjoys a distillery visit becomes a free brand ambassador.

Then, with Ed's blessing, I brought all the top salespeople to visit Scotland to see our distilleries. Chivas Regal was the most important brand in the company, but hardly anyone had been to Scotland. How can you be a strong ambassador for a brand if you don't have the passion and the understanding of the brand and the history behind it? We did all that, and sure enough, it paid off. A few years later, I went to Buckingham Palace, where the Queen presented me—as a representative of Seagram—an award for exports because Chivas Regal was selling more than two million cases a year. My plan was for us to get up to five million cases a year within twenty or twenty-five years, which was possible because we had made the right investment in distilling and laying down long-term stock. Too many people in the financial world in New York and London are greedy and think only in terms of short-term profits. Ed wasn't like that. He was willing to take a long-term view, and that's why he supported me when I asked for the $100 million.

Talk about being willing to take one for the team: at one point when we were focusing on marketing Chivas Regal in China, James flew over to Beijing, donned a Keepers of the Quaich kilt (Keepers of the Quaich is an international society that recognizes those who have shown outstanding commitment to the Scotch whisky industry), and went on television to advertise Chivas Regal. China was an important future market for us because Chinese politics were shifting, capitalism was budding, and eight hundred million people were emerging from poverty. We knew from other global marketing experiences that as soon as a society comes into money, its people start buying more liquor and better liquor, so it was a perfect time for us to be educating Chinese consumers about Chivas Regal. And there was James Espey with his kilt and his medals and his classy accent (he was raised in Zambia and South Africa) on Chinese television, holding a bottle of Chivas Regal and telling the Chinese to "drink better." The message got across loud and clear, and Chivas Regal was soon the top whisky brand in China. It got to 750,000 cases per year a few years ago.

• • •

Having good working relationships is so essential in business. That's true in all industries, but it's especially valuable in the liquor business. People move from one company to another to another, and companies acquire each other or are merged together by larger organizations, such as Diageo, which owns many brands that had once been under Seagram's umbrella. Everybody knows each other in the liquor business—it's really all about relationships. And it's about family, too. You find many families in which generations of fathers, sons, and, increasingly, daughters work together at a company or go off and start their own brand. In my family, both of my sons and my nephew John work in the industry, and for a short time, my daughter, Beth, did also. The liquor business has played a big role in our family, as it has for many other families as well.

ALL IN THE FAMILY

Recently, Andy Teubner, partner and chief operating officer at Ghost Tequila, came to Palm Beach, Florida, for a meeting with me and my son Paul. Paul is a Ghost Tequila investor and a big fan of Andy and the team at Ghost. The three of us got to talking about the Seagram days, and Andy reminded me that his father, Gordon Teubner, had worked at Seagram when I was there. In fact, Andy's family had three generations at Seagram. Today, former Seagram people can be found at just about every successful liquor brand around the world, from the biggest distributors and manufacturers to the tiniest start-ups and craft distillers. Even now, after companies like Seagram have been broken up and sold off and behemoths like Diageo and Pernod Ricard accumulate brands, the liquor industry continues to be quite close-knit and full of family connections. I enjoyed Andy's reminiscences and asked him to share some of them here.

My grandfather started working as a union laborer at Seagram's Calvert Canadian whisky distillery in Relay, Maryland, right after Prohibition, and he eventually worked his way up to union foreman. Maryland has a strong distilling history, and Sam Bronfman, Seagram's founder, set up a Calvert plant there. Now it's a Guinness beer plant. My father started at Seagram in 1965, working nights in the distillery tasting product and growing the yeast in petri dishes for distillation. His sister worked there also as an administrative assistant. My father spent almost all of his career at Seagram and was senior vice president of manufacturing for the Americas when the company was split up in 2001. Then he worked for a few years at Diageo before retiring.

Like my father, I started out at Seagram right out of college, in field sales in Florida. I was hired by Ed's nephew John McDonnell, who is now at Tito's "Handmade" Vodka. My nephew works at Ghost Tequila, the company I run, making him the fourth generation in my family to be in this business. At Seagram, I held positions of increasing responsibility, both domestically and in the Far East, until Seagram broke apart.

I never worked with Ed, but my father had some dealings with him. Ed was very well respected in the industry. He was known for building Seagram and spreading the Seagram brands globally. What Ed McDonnell did at Seagram was to take a good company and make it great. He built the premier spirits company in the world. It wasn't the Bronfmans; it was Ed McDonnell.

Working in this industry kind of gets in your blood. I took a couple of years off to work in sports merchandising. It was fun, and I learned a lot about expanding distribution and so on, but it was nothing like the liquor business. Not because you're out drinking and partying, but because the product that we make is about celebrating and relaxing and having conversations. It brings people together and makes it possible for you to interact with people in different walks of life.

There's a great deal of craftsmanship that goes into distilling—it's not like making Coca-Cola. There's a science to fermentation and aging, and you have to have people who understand the science of distilling. That was my family's background. My father managed the plant in Louisville, Kentucky, for a while, and I remember going to the bourbon aging warehouses that the company owned and climbing through the barrels with my older brother. I'm sure we weren't supposed to do that, but what fun we had climbing three stories to the top of the barrels and opening up the gorge and sniffing the fumes. I fell in love with the distilling process and with Seagram when I went to the plant with my father. I thought I'd work at Seagram for my whole career, like my father and grandfather before me. But that was not to be.

The liquor business is incestuous—a small world. In sales, the conventional wisdom is that you never want to make fun of or overly criticize another brand because you'll probably end up selling it at some point. The brands change hands frequently, and people move around from company to company.

Seagram put so many people into the industry, and we're spread out all over the world. The impact that Seagram has had on the industry overall is amazing—we've had all the top jobs with all the major distilleries, the major suppliers. So many of these companies are run by former Seagram senior executives. Seagram's goal was to be one of the best managed beverage companies, and I think it was. We had phenomenal brands and phenomenal resources because those brands threw off a lot of money. And it really was an incredible place to learn the business—the company believed in investing in people. That's why people stayed there so long. Seagram had very little employee turnover. It wasn't because our salaries were the highest, because they weren't. It was the culture and the training and the leadership and the family environment. If Seagram hadn't broken up, it would be huge now, bigger than Diageo or Pernod Ricard, which dominate the industry today.

It breaks my heart that Seagram broke up. But on the positive side, it enabled all those great people to get out and run companies all over the country, all over the world. Seagram set a standard of craftsmanship, integrity, and tradition. I really value those things, and so did my family. Seagram wasn't just a company—it was my family's history.

Edgar gave me free reign at Seagram. He was totally behind me in everything I wanted to do. When I joined Seagram, the company lacked direction, marketing, and advertising. But my team and I changed that. I wanted to succeed, and everyone who worked for me wanted to succeed. Once we started doing well, we felt inspired to do even better—there's nothing like success to keep people motivated. Within three years of my taking over, Seagram became the largest owner of beverage alcohol brands in the world, thanks in very large part to the company's international growth.

We all felt buoyed by Seagram's success, but I think it was especially gratifying for Edgar. He appreciated the financial rewards, of course, but he also enjoyed the glory that came with them. He relished the attention and praise lavished on him as the CEO of such a high-performing company, perhaps because he had felt so underappreciated by his father. I think it was personal for Edgar, a settling of a score between him and his father, even though Samuel had been dead for years. Seagram's success probably took away some of the sting that had stayed with Edgar since his early years at the company, when he craved, but never received, his father's approval.

"Edgar's shearing emotional experience was being unsure whether his father loved him—and having a father who did not let him run Seagram the way he wanted when he became CEO," wrote Edgar's brother, Charles Bronfman, in *Distilled: A Memoir of Family, Seagram, Baseball, and Philanthropy.*

I enjoyed Edgar's company tremendously, and we became very close friends. Edgar often invited my family and me to Sun Valley, Idaho, where he had a home. My wife and I liked the place so much that we bought a condo there. Eventually I built a family compound in Sun Valley as a surprise for my wife, although she didn't live to see it. When Edgar and I were both in residence in Sun Valley, we'd have lunch together three days a week. It was that close of a friendship.

I was by Edgar Sr.'s bedside in his home in Manhattan when he died in 2013 at the age of eighty-four. I sat with him for the last five days of his life because he didn't want me to go home. I was his closest friend. His death broke my heart—it was a friendship like no other.

● ● ●

I continued to have a hand in the business at Seagram after I retired, remaining as both a consultant to the company and a member of the board of directors for several years. But it was a very difficult time. By then, Edgar's son Edgar Jr., who had taken over as CEO in 1994, had started plunging the company toward what I can only describe as a tragic, spectacular failure. In a very short time, Edgar Jr. would squander most of the successes my team and I had racked up. When I announced my retirement in 1995, the Seagram Spirits and Wine Group had over $5 billion in sales, $700 million in profit, and a $600 million cash flow. But within a few years, most of that had evaporated, and the company would be broken up and sold off at a huge loss. And Edgar Bronfman Jr. would go down in business history as the person who lost Seagram.

As for me, I landed on my feet. I had retired from Seagram, but an exciting new chapter in my international business career was just getting started. Once again, I was thinking big.

6

BUILD A STRONG TEAM

I TALK ABOUT MYSELF A LOT WHEN I DESCRIBE THE ACHIEVE-
MENTS AND ADVENTURES IN MY CAREER. But none of my personal or professional accomplishments could have happened without the
efforts of teams of people who worked with me and supported me. As the
saying goes, no one can whistle a symphony—and believe me, no one can
succeed in business or life without the support of others. Building a strong
team at work and at home is key.

At work, I learned early on that hiring great people is one of the best
ways to ensure success. When you have a fantastic team in place, you can
focus on the big picture, and the people on your team can concentrate on
what they do best, whether marketing or operations or strategic planning.
"I hire people brighter than me, and I get out of their way," Lee Iacocca, the
famed chairman of automaker Chrysler, famously said. That's how I felt
about the people I chose to be on my teams at General Foods, Pillsbury,
and Seagram.

I was lucky enough to have some wonderful teammates over the years. One was Tom Kirchner, who, like me, was a finance guy. We met while working at General Foods, and he was an important part of my team during the Kibon years. A while later, he joined my team at Seagram, where he took care of Latin American markets. He and his lovely wife, Mollie, were neighbors of ours in Hilton Head, and when I left Seagram and started my own international distribution companies, Tom partnered with me and ran the holding company that comprised all of the various distributers. Tom died in 2009 at the age of sixty-eight after a battle with brain cancer.

Since Tom isn't here anymore, I asked Mollie to share some thoughts about our friendship. Not only were Tom and I best friends, but our wives were very close also.

Tom and Ed worked together at General Foods in Rye, New York. Then we moved to Brazil and Tom worked for Ed at Kibon, so I've known Ed a long time. Tom and Ed were very, very close. Thick as thieves. In Rye, they used to play tennis at lunchtime in a nearby club. After going to this club for a long time, they were asked to represent the club in a tennis tournament—but they weren't even members. They had to fess up and admit that they had just been sneaking into the club. Everyone knew them there, but nobody had ever bothered to check to see if they were members. That was the kind of thing that would happen with those two.

After Ed went to Pillsbury, he hired Tom and sent us to Guatemala, Venezuela, and Mexico. Then Ed brought Tom to Seagram, where he ran Tropicana. We started going to Hilton Head in 1972 because of Ed and Kay—we bought a condominium there, and our families would have Thanksgiving together. That's where I live now.

Tom was a very, very bright man and a very levelheaded person. I think Ed appreciated that he was such a good manager. Very easygoing. I was married to him for forty-seven years, and I never saw him lose it. He was bright, he was a very loyal employee, he did his job, and he was a good friend.

One of Ed's best traits is his ability to figure people out and to know if someone is a good person. And Tom was a good person. Ed saw that.

When Tom was dying of brain cancer, caring for him was really hard for me. Toward the end, I couldn't leave him, even though he was under hospice care. The hospice nurses kept telling me to take a break. But I couldn't do it. I wanted to take care of him. One morning, Ed called me and said, "Mollie, let me take you to lunch. You need to get out of the house."

I said, "All right, I'll give you one hour, then I'm going to come right back home." Tom was kind of semiconscious at that point, and I told him I was having lunch with Ed but would be back in an hour. I think Tom must have been waiting for me to get out of that house so he could die. I hadn't even made it to the front gate of this area where we lived when my phone rang and my daughter-in-law told me Tom was gone.

Ed was by my side in a nanosecond, and he stayed with me. He took me to the funeral home and helped me through that whole process. If you are close with Ed, he takes care of you.

Of course, there were times I wanted to strangle Ed. When he was trying to convince us to move to Brazil, he raved about the spectacular weather—he told us it only rained at three o'clock in the afternoon, and after a brief shower, the sun would come out. Well, when we got there, we were staying in a dreadful little hotel with four children under the age of five. There was no playground, no swimming pool, nothing for the children to do—and it rained constantly. I still give Ed a hard time about that little fib.

After Ed left Seagram, Tom worked with him, running the Premier Group in Hilton Head. Tom worked there until the last month before he died. At Premier, they used to have Friday lunches— a bunch of them, probably ten people, would go to lunch together. When the bill came, they would all throw their credit cards in a pile and ask the waitress to pick two to pay the bill. It seemed like Tom's would get picked every Friday. But that's all right. They had so much fun together.

Another incredible teammate was Myron Roeder, who started out as a business connection but soon became one of my best friends. Myron and I worked together at Pillsbury for several years, and when I moved on to Seagram, I hired him to handle our global marketing. He eventually took over as president of Tropicana Products, which Seagram acquired in 1988. Myron was one of the brightest and most understated people I have ever met. Many of the great ideas I put into effect came from the amazing mind of my dear friend Myron. I attribute much of my success to him.

Myron was an incredible thinker. He would gather information and ask everyone their opinion; then he would synthesize it all into a recommendation that would just be spot-on. The amazing thing about Myron, though, was that he was never one to brag about all the ideas he'd come up with. I saw how talented he was and promoted him quickly.

I trusted Myron completely, and I counted on him to be my eyes and ears in the company—not to squeal on people who weren't carrying their weight, but to give me the context and perspective I sometimes couldn't uncover on my own. People tend to hide things from the people in senior positions, either because they're afraid of being blamed for problems or because they want to look smarter than they are. My team understood that I wanted to know about everything, good or bad. Even when I didn't act on information I would hear, I just liked knowing about it.

Myron was such a good friend. He died in 1996 at age sixty-one, and I miss him very much. I asked his wife, Jan, to share a few thoughts about Myron:

Myron and Ed met after Ed started at Pillsbury in Minnesota. Then eventually he joined Ed at Seagram. It was a great opportunity—Myron liked international business, and he was good at what he did. Myron and Ed liked each other very much, and I think Ed appreciated the fact that he knew Myron would be loyal to him.

Myron had a quick sense of humor. He worked well with people and treated them with respect. He wanted to succeed, and he put in long hours and traveled a lot. I think Myron really liked the fact that Ed was a smart businessman. Ed had more of an edge than Myron, which maybe Myron wished he had more of. But they enjoyed each other's company, and there was a lot of laughter when they were together.

Back in the Minnesota days, Ed used to tease me—he knew I loved Minnesota and he would always call it "Minni-no-place."

Myron was diagnosed with colon cancer in the spring of 1995. I loved it that Ed came to see Myron after surgery in November of 1995. Then a few months later, Ed arranged a final trip with the Hilton Head ski group they were part of—they went to Switzerland, and Myron had a wonderful time. Ed was a caring friend. When he spoke at Myron's funeral in December 1996, the pastor limited everyone to three minutes, but Ed, of course, had a lot more to say than three minutes' worth.

Fernando Kfouri is yet another colleague who contributed so much to several of the teams I led. I first met Fernando when I worked at Kibon, where he was the commercial director, and eventually I tapped him to run Seagram's operations in Brazil and then Latin America and North America. (I tried to hire Fernando at Pillsbury after I moved to Minnesota, but he wouldn't even consider it. "I'm from a tropical country," he said. "What am I going to do in the snow? The thought of living in Minnesota scares the hell out of me.") Fernando tells a funny story about meeting me for the first time at Kibon:

One of Ed's financial managers got really upset with me for a sales promotion that I was running. This manager came after me like crazy, and Ed happened to be nearby, close enough to hear the entire conversation—although I didn't know who Ed McDonnell was at the time. I thought my sales promotion was an excellent idea, so I fought back against Ed's financial manager. Ed liked that I was standing up for myself, even though it was his manager that I was standing up to. I think it was the wrong situation but the right start with Ed because he's a fighter, too.

James Espey, another very talented businessman, brought marketing genius to our team at Seagram. As I mentioned earlier, James was the brains behind a strategic marketing plan that gave Seagram a big boost by expanding the Chivas Regal brand into Asia. James is an outspoken guy who doesn't pull any punches, so I asked him to share his view of what it was like working on my team. Here's what he said:

Ed was a good leader because he didn't try to tell you what you should do. His theory was that you cannot keep a pack of dogs and do all the barking yourself. Ed trusted me. When he took me on, he gave me a job, and he let me do it. He brought in other good people, too. And he stopped interference from bureaucrats in New York so they wouldn't get in the way. Ed believed that you should work hard together and then have a drink together—the work was important, but it was always about more than just work. Ed and I both felt the same way about teamwork. In my view, TEAM stands for "together everyone achieves more." Being on a team means thinking "we" rather than "I." As the saying goes, there's no "I" in the word "team."

Marty Bart was another star on my team at Seagram. Marty held a variety of executive positions at Seagram over the years. At one point, he was charged with launching the Captain Morgan brand of products. He came up with some ideas for the launch, and because he was a trusted member of my team, I supported him when he pitched them. I'll let Marty take it from here:

Our rum was up against Bacardi, which was by far the biggest rum out there. We were trying to get some traction in the market. I came up with all these crazy kinds of programs, and we started doing pretty well. But we were losing a lot of money, and this was irritating the board of directors. There was a big meeting about this, and of course Ed was there.

During my presentation, I explained that we had lost $6 million in six months, which sounds awful, but from a sales point of view, we were actually doing quite well. Ed was one of the few executives—in fact, I think he was the only one—who came to my defense. He saw that even though we were losing money, we were getting repeat orders, and retailers were accepting the brand. He understood that when you start a new brand, it costs money and it takes time. You have to invest a lot in a brand to make it successful. Thanks to Ed, I got approval to keep going, and the brand did unbelievably well, in large part because Ed supported me.

When you support your team, they repay you with hard work and loyalty. As Mary Garrard, my secretary at Seagram in London, once said, "If you worked for Ed, you had to work jolly hard. But he rewarded you for that. The fact is, you wanted to work hard for him because he appreciated it. You wanted to be loyal to him."

We worked very hard at Seagram, but we had fun too. My colleague Tony Rodriguez recalls: "We used to have budget meetings in Hawaii because it was a central meeting point for people from New York and Asia. We'd be in meetings all day, and then we'd let loose at night. One time after dinner, Ed and another executive, John Griffin, totally blew everybody away by going backstage and putting on hula skirts. Here are two of the top people at Seagram dressed as two clowns. It was hilarious. The two of them were having a great time, and they got up there and sang and danced with whoever the performer was."

• • •

I often brought people with me as I moved from job to job. Not only did I appreciate how capable they were, but I knew I could trust them. And most of them were a lot of fun, so I knew I enjoyed working with them. Being a successful businessperson requires some very long hours, and surrounding yourself with people you appreciate makes everything easier.

When it came to hiring people and deciding who would perform well on my teams, I tended to trust my gut. I felt that I could size people up pretty quickly, and my first impression usually turned out to be right. As my friend Ken Herich says, "Ed has the ability to size a person up immediately. He knows right away if he likes you or if you're a jackass, and he is usually spot-on."

Over the years, people have told me that they were surprised at how quickly I hired them, preferring to go with my initial reactions rather than multiple levels of long interviews. I never really thought this was unusual, because it typically seemed clear to me right away whether someone was the real deal and worth hiring. But various people, including my friend Peter Schreer from Kibon, have said they look back with surprise when they recall their hiring process with me. Here's Peter's memory:

> The first time I met Ed, in 1971, I was interviewing for a job as data processing manager. At the time, I was working in a similar function at the state university in São Paulo. The first interviewer was the vice president of finance. That went poorly because he spent most of his time asking me all kinds of details about business taxes, with which I was not familiar. The next interviewer was Ed. He asked me how the previous interview went. I told him it hadn't gone well and explained why. Then we chatted comfortably for a while, talking about challenges at Kibon and how I would address them. After about forty minutes discussing his questions in a relaxing way, Ed simply said, "You're hired! Good luck!" I think Ed liked my open feedback about my previous interview, and I felt very comfortable talking with him. The finance VP wasn't happy

with what Ed did, but he was a difficult person to work with. Most managers liked Ed's style, including myself, and emulated it.

Of course, the flip side of the teamwork coin is that when someone on your team isn't working out, you've got to make a change. First you have to work with them to try to address their weaknesses—to change their stripes. But if they're not capable of changing, which is often the case, you have to move them off the team or you risk damaging your team's morale.

Letting people go is never easy, but it's often for the best—not just for the company and the team but for the person who is not performing well. Often a poor performance occurs when an individual and a team are a poor match. Releasing someone from a job in which they're floundering frees them to find an opportunity that better aligns with their skills.

What did I expect from the people on my team? Hard work, of course, as well as ingenuity and resourcefulness. A sense of fun and a willingness to take risks. But I also expected honesty. I had no patience for yes-men and yes-women. If you worked for me and you had an opinion that differed from mine, I expected you to stand up to me, express your opinion, and back it up with facts, data, or a compelling argument for why I should trust your gut more than mine. I didn't always agree with people when they did this or decide to follow their advice, but I always respected them for taking a stand. My Seagram colleague Tony Rodriguez can back me up on this. He tells this story:

One time I was in a meeting with Ed and my boss, an executive who reported to Ed but who really didn't fit in with our team. When the meeting ended and my boss and I got up to leave, Ed said, "Tony, can you stay for a minute?" After my boss left, Ed said to me, "Have you ever noticed that when the three of us are in a room, your boss always agrees with me?" Sure I had noticed—the guy was known for it. "That means one of us must be redundant." At that point, I almost burst out laughing. Ed's face lit up, and he said, "And if one of us is redundant, I don't think it's me." Out of a sense of duty, I tried to stand up for my boss, although I admit that I wasn't especially convincing because I wasn't crazy about the guy either.

"You know, I can tell a tiger by its stripes," Ed said, "and I don't think this one's going to change. So we just have to find a way to deal with this. But we have to be careful, because when trees fall, they land hard." It felt like a scene from *The Sopranos* or *The Godfather*, and there was now a contract out on this guy. I knew Ed was going to find a way to get rid of him, and he did. Within months, the guy had a new assignment that made him happy enough that he didn't even care he was being sidelined. It reminded me of the Churchill quote, "Tact is the ability to tell someone to go to hell in such a way that they look forward to the trip." Ed had the ability to engage in that kind of diplomacy. Once the guy was gone, Ed elevated me to be his top finance person. It was clear to me that he was sending me the message, "I'm counting on you to tell me what I need to hear, not what I want to hear."

I had to be able to trust the people on my team, and the best way to gain my trust was to be honest with me. If you worked for me and I didn't trust you, or if I found out that you had done something behind my back, forget about it—you were finished. It may sound harsh, but it was the only way I could operate.

Building a strong team is an investment in the future as well as the present. Having a good team in place helps ensure that your company can continue to do well after you move on. When I left Seagram, one of the things I was proud of was that I was leaving the company in good hands with the right people in place for succession. I had recruited and developed what I considered to be the most effective management team in the industry.

• • •

One of the most inspiring displays of corporate teamwork I've ever seen occurred in 1973, when a huge fire broke out in the Kibon plant in São Paulo. The fire started early on a Sunday morning in the area of the plant that housed Kibon's chocolate and candy operations, as well as the finished goods warehouse for dry products. (Fortunately, foot-thick firewalls protected Kibon's ice cream manufacturing operations from the blaze, which was very fortunate because ice cream products contributed 70 percent of the company's sales at the time.)

The plant was closed when the fire started, thank goodness, so we knew our employees were safe. But we were very concerned about the plant, which appeared in danger of being completely consumed by flames. Our worries grew when we saw the local fire department making little headway fighting the fire. Very low water pressure—a common problem at the time in São Paulo—and lack of adequate equipment meant the fire quickly overwhelmed the fire department. I felt so completely helpless watching the plant burn.

And then Kibon employees came to the rescue. Word of the fire quickly spread around the community, and even though it was Sunday morning, our workers began showing up by the hundreds. Realizing that the only way to save the plant was to take action themselves, the Kibon workers stepped up in any way they could. Some made use of whatever equipment they could lay their hands on to fight the fire and stop it from spreading. Others managed to locate and help bring in truckloads of drinking water to spray on the flames.

While some employees fought the fire, others volunteered to run into the plant to locate and remove crucial paperwork and to dismantle valuable machinery and equipment, which they carried out to safety. Everyone pitched in, including many women who set up big tables of food for the firefighters and workers.

Fred Miller, our operations manager, helped organize and direct the employee efforts and to make sure everyone stayed safe. Meanwhile, our sales team immediately began notifying all of our retail customers that our Rio de Janeiro plant would be increasing its output to make sure that deliveries of Kibon products would not be interrupted by the fire. Some of our employees worked seventy-two hours straight, helping to fight the fire and salvage material from the plant. Talk about teamwork!

The blaze burned for nearly two days and was finally extinguished when the Brazilian military brought in heavy firefighting equipment.

The teamwork continued once the fire was out. Employees worked overtime setting up shop in other Kibon buildings so we could, as quickly and to the greatest degree possible, return to business as usual while plant repairs and rebuilding took place. During the following months, our workers showed flexibility, professionalism, and ingenuity, making sure the company continued to produce and prosper. I felt so proud of them and very, very thankful for their efforts.

I have no doubt that if it weren't for the dedication of the Kibon employees, the plant would have burned to the ground and been completely destroyed. Instead, they kept damage to a minimum and production stayed mostly online.

With that fire, I saw the power of teamwork. I discovered that if you have the right team in place, you can accomplish nearly anything—even feats that seem at first to be impossible. I never, ever forgot that lesson.

• • •

I owed my success not just to my teams at work but to my family as well. From the earliest days, my wife, Kay, was the most important person on Team McDonnell. Without her support, organizational skills, and hard work, I couldn't have traveled all over the world making business deals and pursuing promotions. Many wives would have said no to international living, which can be tough on spouses. But Kay took it all in stride and did most of the heavy lifting when it came to shouldering the burdens of moving our family, finding schools for our children, and settling us into our new living arrangements. Kay always managed to make us feel at home, no matter where we lived.

Kay also went out of her way to help the other wives who were setting up homes in far-flung locations. "Kay was like my big sister," says Mollie Kirchner, wife of my colleague Tom Kirchner. (While working at General Foods, I brought Tom down to São Paulo to work at Kibon.) "Kay was very good to me. When Tom and I were transferred to Brazil, I had four children under the age of five, including an infant. It was quite a shock to me—there was no baby food, no nothing. Kay was so helpful getting us settled. I'd go to her whenever I had any kind of question, like whether to put my son in nursery school. She was always there for me, and she really knew what she was doing. Her kids were around the same ages as mine, and she'd already been in Brazil for a while, so she knew her way around."

Jan Roeder, wife of my dear friend and colleague Myron Roeder, also remembers Kay with fondness. "I liked Kay because she was a person who would tell it like it was," she recalls. "She knew how to play the businessman's wife, but she kept her feet on the ground. I loved it when she admonished Ed in Portuguese, because of course none of us knew the language and didn't know what she was saying to him. I admired the fact that she could live in Brazil, or wherever it was, and adapt to it. My family moved around in the United States and lived in England twice, but Brazil? I don't know if I could have lived there. We were the kind of friends that could just pick up in the middle of a sentence even if we hadn't seen each other for a fairly long time."

Kay was born in Allston, Massachusetts, in 1935. As I mentioned earlier, her parents, Albert and Catherine McNamara, weren't big fans of mine, but they raised a wonderful woman, so I can't complain about them too much. Kay graduated from Mount Saint Joseph Academy high school in Brighton before earning a degree in early childhood education from Curry College in Milton. After graduation, she taught kindergarten for a short time in Waltham, Massachusetts.

I met Kay in 1955 at a meet and greet on my first day of college. I was a freshman at Suffolk University, and she was a sophomore at Curry College. Like many of our baby boomer classmates in the family-focused 1950s, we married shortly after I graduated from college. (Today, most men and women wait until their late twenties to marry, but back in 1959, couples were more likely to get married in their early twenties.) When I was in college, the standard operating procedure among many of the guys I knew was to meet a girl right at the start of college and marry her right after graduation. That's exactly what I did. Our first child, Ted, was born in 1961, followed by Paul almost two years later, and Beth a couple of years after that.

All of our children were born in Massachusetts, but in 1968, when Beth was just a toddler, we moved to São Paulo so I could take the position at Kibon. My job when we moved to Brazil was to turn Kibon around from loss to profit; Kay's job was to do everything else our family needed.

What a huge task!

Living internationally wasn't all hard work. Kay enjoyed golf and tennis, which we played together in various places across the world. She loved our home in Hilton Head, South Carolina, which we bought in the mid-1970s so we'd have a home base in the States. She also liked going to Sun Valley, Idaho, where we bought a condo in the 1980s after spending time visiting Edgar Bronfman Sr. in his home there.

Around 2005, I began building a large home in Sun Valley as a surprise for Kay. Her health had started to fail, and I wanted her to have a large, luxurious home that would make her happy and have plenty of room for our friends and family to visit. I asked my friend, contractor Ken Herich, to build a big, beautiful house with everything she would need, including an elevator to the bedroom floor, because the Sun Valley altitude made it difficult for her to climb the stairs in our three-story condo. Unfortunately, though, Kay didn't live long enough to see it finished. I still own that home, and when our family gathers there to ski in the winter or enjoy the glorious Idaho summers, I feel so sad to think of everything she's missed out on since her death—not the least of which is seeing her only grandchild, Patrick, grow up. How she doted on him when she was alive. Kay loved being a mother, and she absolutely adored being a grandmother.

Kay was one in a million, and I loved her very much. I was devastated to say goodbye to her in 2012, after fifty-two years of marriage, but I'm so thankful she was surrounded by our family when she passed away.

Today, I'm still lucky to have a tremendous team of loved ones supporting me: my children, Ted, Paul, and Beth; my grandson, Patrick; my sister, Peggy; my brothers, John and Bill, and their families; my now-partner, Hope Lika, and her family; and the many, many friends I have made over the years. No man could ask for a better team.

KAY McDONNELL: THE CAPTAIN OF OUR FAMILY TEAM

My daughter, Beth, was very close to her mother, so I asked her to share some thoughts about Kay and her skill at keeping our family organized while we moved around for my work.

My mother was the epitome of a corporate wife. She was the glue that held our family together. When my father would change jobs, it was her job to find us a new home in a new country, get us enrolled in new schools, supervise the move, and set up a household. She took care of everything and had to juggle so many details. It wasn't until I became a parent when I realized how hard that must have been with the lifestyle we were living, following my father around from place to place. She was moving from country to country with three children, arranging schools, making sure everyone had a stable life, dealing with everyone's problems—it's pretty amazing that she did all that. My father was always working, so she was the one who had to keep everything running smoothly on the home front.

Mother wasn't always comfortable in the role of corporate wife, but she made the best of it. She wasn't someone who liked to go out and spend a lot of money on expensive clothes and things, like some of the other wives. She just wasn't like that. But she had a small circle of very close friends, including Mollie Kirchner and Jan Roeder, other women who were living the same kind of corporate-wife life as my mother. She was the type of person who if she liked you, she really liked you. If she didn't, she'd play the good corporate wife and just put up with you, but that was it.

She was always trying to keep my father grounded. Sometimes he was like a teenager, and she'd have to tell him to stop goofing around. She was the disciplinarian for us kids, and he was all about fun—until it came to academics, and then he got serious. He always put a very high value on academics, probably because he had to work so hard to succeed. If you didn't do well or try hard, he'd get after you. Mother cared about academics too, but it mattered more to him. I'm not sure how smart my brothers and I were, though—we like to say that the brains skipped a generation, because my father had them and my son, Patrick, has them.

My father was always traveling, and my mother would mostly stay home with us, although sometimes she would travel with him. When she did, the hosts would make a big fuss over her because she was the wife of an important executive. My father loved that kind of fanfare, but she didn't care for it.

She enjoyed her life as an international corporate wife most of the time, I think, but when my father retired from Seagram, she was finished with it all. She wanted to settle down in Hilton Head and retire from being a corporate wife, but my father wanted to keep working and traveling. He had no interest in slowing down. So when he started his distribution companies in Asia and the Caribbean, he headquartered them in Hilton Head. She'd mostly stay put while he traveled around running his businesses. It worked for both of them.

Her health started failing when she was still young. She was sick for seven or eight years, and during that time, she was in and out of hospitals and nursing homes. I was living in Hilton Head, so I was her primary caregiver. My father was very loving, but it was terribly difficult for him to see her so ill for so long.

Our mother died in 2012 at the age of seventy-seven, leaving holes in all of our hearts.

7

LISTEN MORE THAN YOU TALK

BUSINESS TEXTBOOKS HAVE A LOT TO SAY ABOUT THE "SOFT SKILLS" IN BUSINESS—SKILLS SUCH AS LEADERSHIP, PERSUASION, PROBLEM-SOLVING, AND CONFLICT RESOLUTION. Certainly, all of these skills are critical for business success, especially when you're engaging in global business. But in my view, the ability to listen well is among the most important skills of all. I've always tried to listen more than I talk because, as the saying goes, you can't learn anything by listening to yourself talk. But you can learn a hell of a lot listening to what other people have to say.

Unfortunately, most business leaders are terrible listeners. I know that from observing others in group settings, and the research backs it up. For example, a 2020 study of fourteen thousand employees around the world found that only 8 percent reported that their leaders practiced this skill well. What a missed opportunity.

Over the years, I've sat in many business meetings marveling at verbose executives who never stop talking. How do they learn anything if they never shut up? They don't seem to realize that one of the best ways to make important, relevant, and sometimes game-changing discoveries is simply to sit back, keep your mouth closed, and listen. It's amazing what other people will tell you when you stop talking long enough to give them the space to speak.

I learned this lesson many times over the years. One time in particular stands out—when I gave the entire Kibon workforce a week off after the Brazilian soccer team won the World Cup in 1970. As you may recall, Fernando, my director of human resources, advised me that giving everyone paid time off to celebrate the World Cup victory would win them over at a time when we just couldn't figure out how to turn the company around. At first, I thought he was crazy, but then I decided that I should listen to him because he knew the workers and their culture far better than I did. Sure enough, he was right, and giving them that week off helped jump-start an important financial turnaround at Kibon.

One of the things I took away from that experience and many others like it was that decisions that work well in one country don't necessarily work well in other countries. Too often Americans blunder into other cultures and make decisions based on what would make sense in the United States rather than the country in which they are doing business. This approach can lead to embarrassment and mistakes, not to mention failed business deals. When you're operating in a place with customs and conventions that are different from your own, do yourself a favor and find people like Fernando who will give you the cultural perspective you need to make the right decisions. And for goodness' sake, when they give you advice, listen to them.

Another story about listening stands out as well—when one of my top stars at Seagram, James Espey, requested a mind-boggling $100 million to market Chivas Regal, as I recounted in chapter 5. My first reaction when I heard that number was to tell him he was out of his mind. But I stopped, considered his explanation, reflected on the successes he'd had elsewhere in his career, and decided that the best thing I could do was follow his recommendation and back him up on his request. One look at the Chivas Regal sales numbers in the following years tells you that James knew exactly what he was doing. And all I had to do to look like a genius was listen to him. For the record, Chivas Regal today sells more than five million cases annually.

My policy was always to hire top people—to surround myself with the very best people I could find—and then listen to their advice. As I said, I wouldn't always take it, but I would always hear them out. And on many, many occasions, I learned from them.

● ● ●

Listening to people goes beyond just paying attention to what they say. It also includes observing what they do and learning from that. I've always tried to learn from others who know more about certain things than I do, and it has almost always paid off. Sometimes this isn't easy to do, especially when you outrank the people who know more than you do. You might feel kind of ignorant and embarrassed when you realize that people below you on the corporate ladder have a better, more complete grasp of some things than you do. But let me assure you, it pays to put your pride aside and just settle down and learn from them. And it also boosts their confidence to see that you believe in them and their knowledge.

That's what happened when I first joined Seagram in 1981. By then, I had accumulated quite a bit of experience in the world of global business. After years of working at General Foods and Pillsbury, I had extensive expertise in the worldwide consumer products business, including acquisitions, operations, and marketing, among other things. But one thing I didn't know much about, from a business standpoint, was liquor. Sure, I knew what I liked to drink, and of course I had studied up on Seagram. But I had a lot to learn about the complexities of the liquor industry and the distribution business. So instead of pretending I knew things I didn't, I turned to Marty Bart, one of the smartest guys I knew at Seagram, and asked him to teach me a few things. I'll let Marty tell that story:

> When Ed started at Seagram, I was in sales, and as such, I had to deal with distributors and retailers. They're a very important part of the liquor industry. Now, Ed didn't know the liquor business, and he was very open about that. But he wanted to learn as much as he could, so to his credit, he asked if he could travel around with me to meet some of these people.
>
> I was pretty impressed when he asked me that. Usually when new people came in to the top positions at Seagram, they wouldn't want to move. They would want to sit at 375 Park Avenue, Seagram's headquarters, and make all these big decisions based on their previous experience at other companies. But that wasn't Ed. He wanted me to take him around and introduce him to everyone so he could ask questions and learn all about the business. So that's what I did. We left New York in a helicopter, and we did the East Coast. Then we took the company plane and went all over the country, and I introduced Ed to as many people as I could. He learned a lot that way, and it made him very comfortable. No other top guy had ever done that.
>
> Most of these distributors were father-son operations that had been in business since Prohibition. They were doing very well

for themselves, and they weren't intimidated by someone new coming in—especially someone they'd never worked with before who was new to the business. When Ed walked in the room, they took him with a grain of salt. Who the hell was he to them? They figured he was just some guy coming in to act like a hotshot and try to tell them what to do. But that's not Ed. He won them over by asking them about their business and listening to their concerns. What a team we were. I opened the door, and he went right in.

Seagram had a function called the Seagram Family Association, which was for the sons and daughters of the owners of distribution companies from around the country. It met once a year at a major resort that Seagram picked, and we'd wine and dine them and have various kinds of business meetings. Ordinarily, people at Ed's level would never come to these events, but for several years, he insisted on going. He loved it—not just because it helped him learn, but because he genuinely enjoyed meeting these people and listening to what they had to say.

Whenever Marty and I reminisce about those days, I'm always astonished when he tells me that I was the only top executive who wanted to travel around with him to meet with distributors and retailers. Why *wouldn't* someone in my position want to do that? The distributors and retailers were the people meeting with customers and selling Seagram products. What a wealth of information they could offer in terms of customer interest, marketing, and street-level feedback—good, bad, and indifferent—on how people felt about our brands. And what a golden opportunity for me to connect with them on a personal level and build relationships that would serve all of us—me, Seagram, the distributors, and the retailers. As I've said before, strong relationships are essential in every business, but they are especially crucial in the small-world liquor business.

Of course, I loved to travel and welcomed the opportunity to get out of the office, especially if it involved going to new places. I would get antsy after too long in an office, and traveling out into the field offered me the double benefit of giving me some space as well as the opportunity to listen to important Seagram stakeholders.

• • •

Too many business leaders think they have all the answers. Not me. Obviously I had some of the answers, or I wouldn't have made it as far as I did. But I was also very aware of the fact that there were plenty of things I didn't know. That's why I hired smart, creative, resourceful people—many of whom I brought with me from company to company. Other executives at Seagram and elsewhere also hired good people, but too many of them wouldn't shut their mouths long enough to listen to what their people had to say. As Apple founder Steve Jobs used to say, "It doesn't make sense to hire smart people and then tell them what to do; we hire smart people so they can tell us what to do."

I was always asking people what we could do differently to make things work better. This started at Kibon, after employees thankful for a week off after the World Cup victory began flooding me with excellent advice. And it continued throughout my career. When I traveled around the United States with Marty Bart meeting with distributors and retailers, I'd always ask them what we could do differently at Seagram. Often the smallest suggestions would lead to significant adjustments in how we did business.

Companies love to hire high-priced consultants to advise them on strategy. Seagram did this on several occasions. There can be value in this; sometimes consultants delivered decent recommendations that helped us

Edward F. McDonnell '59

Traveling Agent

He is a candid man, Edward F. McDonnell 59 BSBA (with a Suffolk honorary doctorate in commercial science conferred in 1984). He might well have become chief executive officer of the Pillsbury Company, he told an SOM audience on September 25, but found himself homesick for the faster pace and greater heterogeneity of the east coast.

Instead, McDonnell is President of Seagram International, which he joined in 1981 as a vice president, and a member of the board of directors of Joseph E. Seagram & Sons. McDonnell will never be CEO or chairman of the world's largest wines and spirits company. Seagram is a family-owned concern, headed by Edgar M. Bronfman, and there are younger Bronfmans coming along. McDonnell makes the statement matter-of-factly, even, perhaps, serenely. This is a man who knows who he is.

Even the sketchiest description of McDonnell's job reveals manifold responsibilities. As President of Seagram International, he is responsible for twenty-nine operating companies and all Seagram activities outside North America. (The parent company is, of course, Montreal-based, while much of the multinational's business is conducted from one of Manhattan's best-regarded and "newer" skyscrapers on Park Avenue.) The twenty-nine companies reporting to McDonnell are located in twenty-four countries on six continents, with five thousand employees and two hundred brands of wines and spirits—which account for approximately half the parent company's total revenue. Seagram's sales also account for seventy-nine per cent of the spirits market world-wide. (Europe alone was responsible

for $650 million in sales last year.)

McDonnell's 1959 Suffolk Yearbook, of which he was co-editor (and Class President) predicted his future as "Traveling Agent." As yearbook predictions go, it has proven remarkably apt. He and his family have lived overseas for a total of ten years, for seven of which he was President of General Foods' Brazilian subsidiary. The other three years, sometimes broken by stateside assignments, were spent in Europe. He smiles broadly when he mentions England. Home at present is in Manhattan's Sutton Place and Hilton Head, South Carolina, with, one gathers, plenty of overseas travel thrown in. To take him at his own word, only the spell in Minneapolis made him feel a stranger in a strange land.

The title of his lecture that September afternoon was "Financial and Political Risk Factors in International Business." Clearly there are large, even formidable risk factors in doing business overseas. McDonnell readily admits that Seagram's performance in Latin America has frequently been hampered by political and military unrest—although the market has by no means disappeared. Meanwhile, Seagram International is experiencing a thirty-five per cent annual growth—despite the fact that the American dollar has recently declined in competition with other currencies.

Those who (in common with this writer) had not done their homework were somewhat startled to learn that Chivas Regal is Seagram's most prestigious product, its flagship label Scotch. (Glen Grant, Passport, 100 Pipers and Glenlivet Single Malt are also Seagram products.) One tends to associate the Seagram name with Canadian rye whiskeys

In the evening when we were kids, my mother would play the accordion, and we all sang Irish songs.

I was fortunate to be selected to attend the coveted Boston Latin School. That was a game-changing experience because I was invited to friends' homes in more fortunate areas I never dreamed of living in. I knew from that moment I wanted to be successful.

I learned strong leadership skills during my time in the Army.

After a strong high school education at the Boston Latin School, I attended Suffolk University on the GI Bill. I majored in business administration, but somehow my yearbook entry had me as an aspiring travel agent.

MC DONNELL, EDWARD
22 George St.   Hyde Park, Mass.

MAJOR: Management
WHO'S WHO
Activities: President, Senior Class; Assistant Editor, Yearbook Staff; Veteran's Club — Vice President; Business Club — Class Representative; Newman Club Member; Student Council.

Future: Traveling Agent   Degree: B.S.

"And gladly would he learn and gladly would he teach."

I received an Honorary Doctorate from Suffolk University in 1984. A very proud day for me.

Mr. and Mrs. Albert J. McNamara
request the honour of your presence
at the marriage of their daughter

Catherine Rita

to

Mr. Edward Francis McDonnell

on Saturday, the eighteenth of July
Nineteen hundred and fifty-nine
at two o'clock
Saint Mary of the Nativity Church
Scituate Harbor, Massachusetts

I got married right after college and honeymooned in Bermuda.
That's what everyone did in those days.

Within several years I was sent to Brazil to
troubleshoot Kibon, the worst-performing
business in the entire portfolio of General
Foods. Here I am with the Kibon
Management Team, São Paulo. A year
later, I became President.

NEW PRESIDENT
Edward F. McDonnell (l.) was elected Director President of
Kibon S.A. in the November meeting of directors and shareholders. Pictured with McDonnell are D.K. Evans (c.), General Foods Vice President and President of their Latin American and Pacific operations, and Geofrey Westrop(r.) former
Director President of the Brazilian subsidiary who has been
transferred to London.

McDonnell elected Kibon president

INTERNATIONAL

CREATING A WORLD OF GOOD FOODS

The 3,000 people working at Pillsbury's international subsidiaries around the world made a major contribution in fiscal 1978. Operating profits in F'78 were approximately 40 percent higher than in the previous year. This excellent performance represents continued strong profitability of Erasco, Mocama (Milan) and the minority investments and the initiation of successful revitalization programs at H. J. Green's and Gringoire/Brossard. Interim results for fiscal 1979 indicate a continuation of the profit trend established in fiscal 1978. As this magazine went to press, operating profits were well ahead of last year with all major groups (European Grocery, Canada and Latin America/ Pacific contributing to this growth.

Erasco people in West Germany strengthened their No. 1 position in the canned dish-ready meal market in F'78, moving from a No. 3 place four years ago. This company has also achieved a strong No. 2 position in the canned gourmet soup category. The firm has made substantial capital investments in both buildings and equipment in the past five years and is now diversifying into non-canned prod-

Surrounded by foods made by Pillsbury people at subsidiaries in 11 countries is Ed McDonell who was named group vice president-International in the Fall of 1978.

All together during my career we lived for over twenty years in London. It was a wonderful time. First with General Foods, then Pillsbury, and again with Seagram. Kay and I loved living there, and the kids loved it, too.

Me, when I was young.

Seagram sponsored many of the most prestigious events around the world. Here we are at the Grand National with Margaret Thatcher.

I was on the board for Carnegie Hall. Here I am with Michael Douglas and Edgar Bronfman Jr. Our board meetings were held on the stage of Carnegie Hall–quite a setting for a board meeting.

The Keepers of the Quaich is an international society that recognizes those who have shown outstanding commitment to the Scotch whisky industry. Founded by the leading distillers, it is by its very nature the beating heart of the industry. I was the proud recipient at the meeting in Scotland with Ronald Reagan in attendance.

With Edgar (center), James Espey (far right), and other associates at Barton & Guestier in Bordeaux, France.

Hans Denecki, head of our German company, often joined us for a ski trip in St. Moritz with my two sons, Ted and Paul.

We never stopped mixing business and fun in St. Moritz.

Our US home base was in Hilton Head Island, South Carolina, where we spent most summers and vacation time.

My son, Ted, and his wife, Terry, were married in the US Virgin Islands.

June 25

Dear Ed –

I know this is not the exact date, but nevertheless you and we are celebrating 10 years that you have been with Seagram.

I not only congratulate you, I congratulate us. You, and thus we, have gone from strength to strength. Your numbers, and thus our numbers, speak for themselves. The fact that you have recently been asked to accept the challenge of running our wine and spirits businesses world-wide speaks for itself, too.

Some of my treasured memories are personal notes from Edgar Sr. Here is a note of congratulations on my tenth year at Seagram.

On a personal note, you are fun to work with. Your great success is probably due to the fact that you are also fun to work for (although I can't personally attest to that, but there are many who can).

Like any successful marriage, we have been good for each other. You have really understood Seagram and what it means, and more, you have expanded that meaning with your sincerity, hard work, and devotion to all who are involved with you.

God bless, Edgar

The Seagram Company Ltd.

1430 PEEL STREET, MONTREAL, QUEBEC, CANADA H3A 1S8

CO-CHAIRMAN

October 12, 1993

Mr. Edward F. McDonnell
375 Park Avenue
New York, N.Y. 10152-0192

Dear Ed:

My heartiest congratulations!! I have some idea of how much time, effort, and brainpower went into the securing of the Absolut contract, but really have no idea of the emotional ups and downs that were ever-present on this long and arduous journey. The successful conclusion of the voyage speaks volumes about the kind of organization you have built over the years. Saying that "we are number one" is one thing - proving it to a dispassionate potential supplier with all that was at stake is quite another.

Today is a really good day for Seagram. You deserve all the plaudits that will come your way.

Well, well done, Ed.

Best.

Charles.

Charles R. Bronfman

The real highlight of my career was the purchase of Absolut vodka from the Swedish government. It was quite a win for Seagram!

The President and Mrs. Clinton
request the pleasure of your company
in celebration of Ireland to be held at
The White House
on Thursday, March 17, 1994
at seven-thirty o'clock

Black Tie

Much to my surprise, I was honored at the White House as Irish Businessman of the Year in 1994. I remember stealing napkins for my kids as keepsakes.

SEAGRAM'S
INTERNATIONAL STRATEGY

> "Seagram is becoming a stronger force within the total industry in terms of discipline, focus, goals and objectives."
>
> *Ed McDonnell*

Myron Roeder, president, Seagram Europe, and I were the best of friends. We shared the same vision for the company, and we enjoyed life to the fullest.

My retirement from Seagram was bittersweet, although I had much lined up for my future years owning several distribution facilities in the Caribbean and Asia.

At my retirement party at the Four Seasons, we celebrated, and Edgar Sr. and I knew we would remain the best of friends forever. And we did. And to this day, I remain in touch with many of the wonderful people that worked with me.

Below is a copy of the touching speech delivered by Edgar Jr.

On a far less somber note, tomorrow, the 1st of June, marks an important day in the history of the Seagram Company. Tomorrow is the day on which Edward F. McDonnell officially steps down as President of The Seagram Spirits And Wine Group. He will remain as both a consultant to Seagram as well as a member of our Board of Directors and in both capacities, we will continue to rely on his talent and advice.

However, I cannot let this moment pass without a tip of the hat to Ed McDonnell and his extraordinary achievements. When Ed joined Seagram in 1981 as President of our international operations, we were principally a North American company with almost 100% of our profitability coming from that area. Today we are truly a global company, with almost 80% of our profitability coming from markets outside North America. The worldwide organization that has been built, generally acknowledged as being the finest in the spirits and wine industry, was built principally by Ed. The brands, the people, the profits, are the result of Ed's vision, determination and talent. Ed's contribution to Seagram is incalculable, including building a management team that will carry on and further expand our businesses throughout the world. On behalf of our Board, and with deep personal gratitude for all he has meant to me, both as my boss and later as my colleague, I would like to ask Ed to stand and be recognized for his outstanding record of achievement.

(212) 572-7599
FAX (212) 572-7213

The Seagram Spirits And Wine Group

EXECUTIVE OFFICES
375 PARK AVENUE • NEW YORK, NY 10152-0192

EDWARD F. McDONNELL
PRESIDENT

February 21, 1995

Dear Edgar:

Now that I've had several days to recover from the shock of last Wednesday evening's festivities, I want to take a moment to thank you from the bottom of my heart. You really now how to make a person feel proud.

Edgar, over the past 14 years through the good times and tough times (never bad) you have always been the visionary, advisor and counselor on our worldwide business building efforts. You, Efer and I have been a wonderful business building team and the results speak for themselves.

On a personal note, over the same period, you have always been a great friend and supporter especially when I needed you and when I thought my world was caving in (Lou Goldberg/David Sacks)--those were the tough times. Without you I couldn't have survived.

Edgar, you are an extraordinarily special human being, a wonderful friend and, equally important, a great guy to share a few drinks with--I love you. I know I'll be around for a long time to come and I look forward to continuing our special relationship.

Sincerely,

Mr. Edgar M. Bronfman
375 Park Avenue
New York NY 10152

My post-retirement reply to Edgar Sr.

I continue to give back to Suffolk. Here I am with my son, Paul, and grandson, Patrick, when the university honored me at the McDonnell International Scholarship Fund luncheon in 2019. One of my greatest pleasures is meeting some of the students who have benefited from the fund I set up. They are an inspiration.

Only in New York. Hope Lika and I lived in the same building and rode the same elevator for twenty years before we actually met four years ago and started dating. Every day is a great adventure with her. It was Hope's idea for me to write this book.

I split my time currently between New York City, Hilton Head Island, and Sun Valley, Idaho. I owe it to Edgar, who urged me to come out to Sun Valley to ski. On my first day here, I fell in love with the place.

Here I am enjoying my backyard, and I toast Edgar Sr. on many a night.

Something I learned from an early age and will never forget:

The harder you work, the luckier you get.

out. But I have to tell you, I usually got the best guidance from the people I worked with. They're the ones who really understood our company, customers, and business. It's amazing how much wonderful advice you can receive simply by asking people for it—and then listening to what they say. Sometimes people with amazing advice are just waiting to be invited to offer guidance. If nobody asks, they keep it to themselves. Put your pride aside and ask for their recommendations! Getting advice from your own people is a lot cheaper than hiring million-dollar consultants.

Tony Rodriguez, an important member of my team at Seagram, sums up my approach to listening:

> Many times Ed told us, "I want to hear your viewpoint. We won't always agree—I may not change your mind, and you may not change mine, but I am listening to you. Once I make a decision, we'll need to move forward and do the best we can. But we're in it together." I wish there were more of that in business.

Listening well also allows you to ask game-changing questions. Over the years, I've seen too many executives hold back on asking questions. Perhaps they didn't want to look ignorant, or perhaps they felt that asking questions would make them seem as if they weren't in control of the conversation. But again, why hire brilliant people if you're not going to ask them to contribute their knowledge and expertise?

I've talked about this approach a fair amount with my friend Stephen Herbits, who held several positions at Seagram, including executive vice president of corporate policy and external affairs. As a former consultant to several secretaries and deputy secretaries of the US Department of Defense, Steve certainly knows a few things about being diplomatic. Here are some of his recollections about how this played out for us at Seagram:

I never reported to Ed, but I saw him in action in a lot of meetings. He had a sort of old-country style. He never raised his voice. He was always very strategic, very tactical. Sometimes he would stand in front of a room and talk, and it would almost sound like he didn't know what he was talking about. But when you listened closely, you realized he was four steps ahead of everyone else the whole time.

When Ed responded to something someone else said, he would often do it in question form rather than assertion form. And there was no edge to his questions. Instead of saying "We're going to do this, we're going to do that," he'd say, "What if we did this? What if we did that?" And instead of asking those questions in a brittle, assertive way, he'd ask them in a supportive, curious way. Of course, when he asked questions, he usually already knew the answers. But by communicating in that way, he allowed his people to feel that they were part of the decision rather than feeling that a decision was being forced on them.

There are many executives—and I'm probably one of them—who would listen to people and then just make a unilateral decision. But Ed wasn't like that. I always envied what I thought of as his soft diplomatic skills.

I had a friend who was a semiprofessional tennis player, and when I played tennis with her, she would never criticize me even though she was a much better player. I asked her about that once, and she said, "Criticizing you would just reinforce something you're doing wrong. I'd rather tell you when you're doing something right and reinforce that. And sometimes I make a suggestion about how you can do something differently, but I don't want to reinforce your mistakes." That style blew my mind, and it helped me become a much better tennis player.

Ed's style was like that, too. He would reinforce the positive and, when necessary, use questions to bring someone around to his way of thinking. I never heard him say, "That's a dumb idea." I did that sometimes myself, and it was rarely the right tactic. I'd often end up apologizing.

I think the principle I took from those conversations was, you don't shout at the person you're trying to persuade, you encourage them. That was Ed's style. It was so inherent in his success and something that I've always admired and valued, even though I wasn't necessarily able to do it myself.

Listening to people helps build their trust in you. When they see that you are open to what they are saying, their confidence in you grows. Their willingness to take risks in their communication with you increases, too. I can't tell you how many times a brilliant idea came about after someone on my team started off by saying, "This may sound crazy, but . . ." An environment of trust and safety allows creativity and inventiveness to flourish because people feel comfortable introducing ideas that are occasionally so crazy that they're brilliant. So make yourself approachable—when you do, people will trust you with their best ideas.

One of the most important pieces of advice I can offer to people who are trying to build a career in business is to stop thinking you're so smart that you can't learn from anyone else. You're not—or you shouldn't be. If you're always the smartest one in the room, and if the people in the room are all people whom you've hired, you're not hiring the right people. You'll serve yourself and your organization best if the people on your team bring skills and knowledge you don't possess. Hire brilliant people, listen to them, and learn from them.

That's not saying you can slack off when it comes to educating yourself about your business, your competitors, and the people with whom you will be negotiating. Absolutely not. Although you should be hiring brilliant people, you should also hold yourself up to a standard of brilliance, hard work, and preparation. Expecting as much from yourself as you do from others will take you a long way in your business career.

LISTENING AND LEARNING

I was honored when my friend, Hope Lika, offered to share some thoughts about the importance I place on listening.

Ed and I met a few years ago, so I didn't know him when he was at the height of his business career. But I see how he treats people in his everyday life now, and I recognize that one of the reasons he was so successful in business is because he's a great listener.

I worked in advertising for many years, and it was a frenetic and competitive environment filled with high emotions, creative sensitivities, and continuous deadlines. Everybody, client and coworker alike, was always on edge. Just out of college and a newbie in the firm, I came to realize that the three-martini lunches between executives and clients set the stage for winning an account, but the real work was done by us minions into the wee hours of the night. It took quite a while for me to realize I needed to find the tools necessary to move up from worker to executive. The top brass hardly appreciated the worker bees as they should. Creative people move to their own drum and, by nature, just aren't wired to work in collaborative teams.

But Ed doesn't operate that way. He is a master of putting people together for the good of the goal. He listens to people and is patient—he just knows how to make people feel important. Ed has an innate sense of who meshes and who doesn't. He knows who can lead and who is the best follower to make something happen. Very early on in a relationship, he understands what someone's strong points are, and he learns from them. I'm amazed by that skill. And I have such respect for Ed because he still uses that approach in his everyday life. When Ed listens or speaks, he actually looks you in the eye! It's such a comforting feeling, and to me, it displays such strength and confidence. When he meets people, he wants to learn about *them* and hear *their* stories. Who listens like that anymore? Most people don't even listen to their spouses.

I've asked Ed about it and he says, "Why wouldn't I listen? I have so much to learn from people." He never wants to go even a single day without learning new things and meeting new people. I've walked into stores with him, and I'm so surprised to see that all the workers know him. He says hello to everyone he meets—he can't even imagine getting into an elevator without greeting every single person in it. When he walks down the street and sees someone approaching, he says hello. It just comes naturally to him.

His entire approach to business was kindness, listening to others rather than trying to be a know-it-all himself. I've never heard him raise his voice. Not once. That's who he is.

We often share stories about the brands Ed ran and the advertising business—I worked on several food and spirits accounts over the years. He worked very hard and at lightning speed, but he always saw a way to include fun. He was a powerhouse and still is very much so. Ed makes the most of life and inspires me every day.

8

KNOW WHEN IT'S TIME TO WALK AWAY

IT WAS 1995, AND I WAS A FEW MONTHS AWAY FROM MY SIX-TIETH BIRTHDAY. I certainly wasn't ready to end my career, but I didn't want to stay at Seagram. I wasn't having fun anymore—I'd had enough. It was time for me to walk away from the best job I ever had.

People seeking business advice often ask me about how to know when it's time to walk away from a negotiation, from a job, from a struggling business, from a dream. Everyone wants to be persistent, to persevere through challenges, and to climb over obstacles. Your whole life you've succeeded by pushing yourself past all kinds of barriers and roadblocks. You think of yourself as a winner, not a quitter. But sometimes quitting is the best choice.

How do you know when it's time to double down and when it's time to walk away? For me, the answer always lies in my gut. Call it intuition or instinct if you'd like. Or maybe it's some kind of inner wisdom. I think of it as a feeling that shows up in my gut and stays there, waiting for my brain to discover it. I don't always want to believe what my gut is telling me, and sometimes my mind works very hard to ignore it. But it's there. And it's usually always right. I rarely go wrong when I follow my gut.

During my last year or two at Seagram, my gut had a lot on its mind. It was telling me to walk away from all the BS going on at the top of the company. My brain didn't want to listen because I'd achieved so much and still saw a huge amount of potential for myself and the company. But too many things had changed. I felt frustrated and annoyed. Now that Edgar Bronfman Jr. had taken over as CEO and was calling the shots at Seagram, the company was moving in a direction that not only strayed from its core business but seemed unlikely to lead to success. Some days it felt as if Seagram were a ship that was speeding toward a gigantic iceberg that would break the company apart. And, unfortunately, the ship was being piloted by a very inexperienced captain: Edgar Bronfman Jr.

Finally I listened to my gut and decided it was time for me to leave.

● ● ●

Edgar Bronfman Jr. was the second son born to Edgar Sr. and his first wife, Ann Loeb. After a brief, unsuccessful attempt at producing movies, Edgar Jr. accepted his father's invitation to join Seagram in 1982, which was the year after I had been hired. Junior was twenty-seven at the time. (Note: To distinguish clearly between the two Edgars in this story, I refer to Edgar Sr. as "Edgar" and Edgar Jr. as "Junior.") According to financial journalist Nicholas Faith, author of the book *The Bronfmans: The Rise and Fall of the House of Seagram*, Edgar, who had recently been appointed president of the World Jewish Congress and was looking to reduce his commitment to Seagram, "startled" Junior by asking him to come and work for Seagram. Junior's acceptance of the offer "was clearly influenced by the fact that his showbiz career was not getting anywhere, but he probably also felt his tribal roots," Faith wrote.

Other than growing up in the Bronfman family, Junior had no experience whatsoever in the liquor business. He hadn't even gone to college; according to his father, Junior considered college a waste of time. However, Edgar had always been dazzled by what he saw as his son's innate business sense. Ever since Junior, whom friends and family referred to as Efer, was a teenager, it was clear to Edgar, as he wrote in his book *Good Spirits*, that "the brilliant, tough-minded businessman in our family would be Efer. He is one of those rare individuals who instinctively understands the business world and always has his priorities in order."

Three months after Junior started working at Seagram, Edgar promoted him to head Seagram Europe. You would think that as president of Seagram International, I would have been involved in deciding who would run Seagram Europe or that I would at least have known about Edgar's plan to give that job to Junior. But you would be wrong. I found out about Junior's promotion to the top position in Seagram Europe on the company plane while flying to London with Junior and some other Seagram people. Believe it or not, I was on my way to London to start my search for a new president of Seagram Europe. I mentioned this to Junior while in flight, and he said, "Didn't my father tell you? I'm going to run Europe."

No, Edgar hadn't mentioned that to me. And if he had asked me for my opinion, I would have told him Junior was nowhere near ready to head up Seagram Europe.

In Europe, Junior was supposedly working for me; I was told to show him the ropes, so to speak. We got along fairly well at first; Junior worked hard and seemed to want to learn the business. He could be a very likable guy when he wanted to be. And I'll be honest: certain acquisitions that I wanted to make won approval faster with the top brass at Seagram because

Junior was attached to them. But despite Junior's attempts at learning the business, too often he was in over his head.

In 1984, Edgar brought Junior back to the United States to run the House of Seagram, the company's domestic sales business, which at the time was Seagram's largest division.

Then, in 1986, a bomb dropped. Without alerting his top people at Seagram—including his own brother, Charles—Edgar made public his intentions to elevate Junior to the top Seagram management position at some point in the future.

As Charles tells it in his book *Distilled*, "In an interview with *Fortune* in 1986, without having informed the board or me—his partner—Edgar announced to the world that Edgar Jr. would eventually be his successor as CEO of Seagram." Charles was running Seagram's Canadian business at the time, and as Edgar's younger brother, he certainly should have been considered for the CEO position when Edgar stepped aside.

Seagram watchers were also surprised that Edgar's oldest son, Sam, was not considered. But Edgar never really thought of Sam as successor material. "This in no way reflects poorly on Sam, as I later told him," Edgar wrote. "But my responsibility was to choose the right CEO for Seagram regardless of presumed birthright or familial relationship." Edgar truly felt that by choosing Junior to take over, he was making the best choice for everyone involved. "All my life I have believed that the job of CEO is to optimize the value of the business for the benefit of the shareholders, whether those shareholders are family or strangers," Edgar wrote in his book. "And to do this, the CEO has to choose the most qualified people for the task, inside the family or out. To quote *The Godfather*, this was business."

With that announcement made, Junior continued to take on more responsibility. In 1989, Edgar named Junior Seagram's president and COO.

And then in 1994, he gave Junior the top job of CEO. Edgar, who was sixty-five, would remain at the company as executive chairman, but Junior was running the show.

Although I shouldn't have been shocked when Edgar put Junior in charge of Seagram, the news shook me. Junior had no business running the company. And I'll be honest: I did not like the idea of having to report to a kid who knew far, far less about the business than I did.

I remained at Seagram for about a year after Junior took over as CEO. I tried to stay focused on organizing Seagram holdings in Asia and the Caribbean, but I knew Junior's elevation to CEO was the beginning of the end for me. I found it impossible to wall myself off from what was going on with Junior. I felt so frustrated by Junior's decisions and, perhaps even more, by Edgar's support of his less-than-qualified son. Unfortunately, Junior was far more interested in the entertainment business than the liquor business. What's more, he had little interest in investing the money we needed to continue growing Seagram's international liquor business. Much of the money earned by our successful liquor brands was going right out the door to Hollywood.

I'm not saying Junior never made a good decision; in fact, he was smart enough to recognize my nephew John McDonnell's talent and helped launched John's successful international career. I'll let John tell that story:

I was sent to Taiwan in the mid-1990s. The buzzword then was "reengineering," and I led a team to reengineer our business in Taiwan. I came back and made a presentation to the board of directors at Seagram headquarters. I told them what they had to do to fix all the various problems we were having in Taiwan. And Edgar Bronfman Jr. looked at me and said, "Do you believe everything you just told us?"

And I said, "Yes, absolutely. This is the way to go."

So he said, "Well, if you believe in it so much, then you can move to Taiwan and implement it."

Then I called my wife and said, "Hey, do you want to go on a little journey together?" Luckily, she said yes.

Despite some successes, everything started to fall apart soon after Junior became CEO of Seagram. In 1995, Seagram sold its 25 percent interest in DuPont, whose earnings had been contributing enormous profits and cash flow since 1981. Seagram sold the DuPont shares for somewhere in the neighborhood of $8.8 billion, which sounds like a lot but really should have been more. Soon after, Seagram bought MCA, which owned Universal Pictures movie studios, Universal Studios theme parks, a book publisher, and some television studios, among other things. It also acquired the recording company PolyGram just before the music industry was decimated by start-ups such as Napster that made it simple for people to download music from the internet without paying for it. Seagram took on a huge amount of debt to finance these purchases. Although Junior felt these acquisitions would move Seagram into the future, none of them made sense to me.

Edgar wanted me to remain at Seagram when Junior took over as CEO. After Seagram bought Universal, I remember Edgar saying to me, "Ed, go out to Los Angeles and tell me what we bought out there." I flew out and met with Ronald Meyer, a high school dropout and talent agent whom Junior had hired to run Universal at a yearly salary of $10 million. "Please tell me what it is you know about this business that you rate a $10 million base salary," I said to Meyer.

And he gave me a very honest answer: "I haven't got a clue. But if

Edgar Bronfman Jr. wants to pay me that money, I'll take it."

Then, in 2000, Seagram sold itself to French conglomerate firm Vivendi in a controversial all-stock acquisition deal. Much has been written about this fiasco, and I have no interest in going into great detail about it here—suffice to say that it was a complete disaster. Junior was named executive vice president of Vivendi Universal, but he had little control over the decisions that followed and was soon relieved of his position. Vivendi CEO Jean-Marie Messier, who had Junior wrapped around his little finger, made a series of idiotic decisions that caused the company to start hemorrhaging money almost immediately, causing the stock price to plummet by 71 percent. Vivendi soon sold off much of Seagram's liquor business to our competitors, Pernod Ricard and Diageo, and auctioned off the famed Seagram art collection in 2003 to pay off debts.

In just a few short years, much of what the Bronfman family had worked for—and what I had worked for at Seagram—was gone. Seagram was broken up and sold for scrap.

Junior received severe criticism for losing the company. "That deal went down as one of the worst mergers in history," wrote business journalist Andrew Ross Sorkin in the *New York Times* in 2008. "He earned a reputation as a star-struck rich kid who made one bad deal after another. *New York* magazine famously called him 'possibly the stupidest person in the media business.' Ouch." In *The Bronfmans*, Nicholas Faith called the Vivendi-Seagram deal "one of the biggest losses ever sustained by a single family."

I will never understand why Edgar supported Junior on his disastrous decisions, but he did. With Edgar's approval—or at least with his failure to step in and say no to Junior's schemes and acquisitions—Junior destroyed a company that had been in the Bronfman family since 1928. Within a few short years, Seagram went from being the most cash-rich company on the New

York Stock Exchange to being almost bankrupt. It was beyond heartbreaking.

According to *Forbes*, the Bronfman family lost about $3 billion during Junior's time as Seagram CEO. "Incredibly, for the first time in my life, I thought I might be headed for insolvency," Edgar's brother Charles wrote in *Distilled*. "A bankrupt Bronfman! Now that would have been one for the history books. My net worth never recovered, although fortunately it's still substantial. Aside from my family's losses, there were Seagram's other shareholders, executives, or anyone in the company who had stock options. All took a terrible hit."

I'm one of the shareholders Charles was describing. I lost money—and plenty of it—due to the ill-fated Vivendi deal. Edgar had promised me during our first meeting that if I did well by him, I'd be comfortable for the rest of my life. Well, I certainly have been comfortable, but I would have been a lot more comfortable if Junior hadn't stepped in and drained away all the profit that we had piled up during my years growing Seagram. I'm certainly not complaining—Seagram paid me nicely. However, I did lose out on more than $50 million when the price of Vivendi stock plummeted. That loss was especially frustrating because, sensing that the stock was about to fall, I decided to exercise my stock options and cash out—but I didn't, because when I mentioned my intentions to Edgar, he convinced me not to do it. And then he sold his Vivendi stock the very next week.

What bothers me more than losing out on that money is the fact that Junior squandered the success that my team and I had worked so hard to achieve during my years at the company. All that work, all those triumphs, flushed down the drain.

"Seagram was the biggest, baddest liquor empire on the face of the earth," says my nephew John McDonnell, who worked at Seagram from 1983 to 2002, eventually reaching the level of executive vice president. "And then Edgar Bronfman Jr. just screwed it up. You can quote me on that."

Most people who hear this story are surprised to find out that throughout all this, Edgar and I remained friends. Looking back, I almost find that hard to believe myself. But we did. I can't really explain it, but our friendship carried us through those difficult years.

Edgar was a proud person, and he truly believed in his son, even though very few people around him, including his own brother, shared that confidence. (Years later, Edgar publicly apologized to Charles for treating him poorly and neglecting to consult with him on major decisions.) But Edgar's faith in his son represented an enormous blind spot in an otherwise intelligent, business-savvy man. I think Edgar's willingness to believe in Junior may have come from the sense he had that his own father, the mercurial Samuel Bronfman, never truly believed in Edgar or gave him the credit he deserved for his work at Seagram while Samuel was still alive. Whatever the reason, Edgar's lapses in judgment with Junior had devastating consequences for Seagram, the Bronfman family, and many Seagram employees and former employees, including me.

Many of us in the Seagram family saw Junior's weaknesses. As my Seagram colleague James Espey has said, "Bronfman Jr. wanted to be the hero. He wanted to be the king." But Edgar didn't see any of that. Junior, who was as well known for his giant ego as for his poor judgment, had fooled his father. Edgar certainly wasn't the first parent in a family business empire to overestimate a child's abilities and underestimate his flaws. But with so much at stake, Edgar's misjudgment stands out as one of the more significant in recent memory.

Eventually Edgar came to recognize Junior's failures, although by then Seagram had been lost. About ten years after Seagram's sale, Edgar admitted to me that he had mishandled the company's transition. I could see how much it hurt him to admit this. As much as I wanted to say, "I told you so," I couldn't do that to my friend. So I said nothing.

But I did shake his hand to acknowledge what had to be a very difficult admission.

WORTH REMEMBERING

When I announced my retirement from Seagram in 1995, I received many kind notes from people with whom I had worked, both at Seagram and other organizations. I've held on to them over the years and occasionally reread them. Here are some excerpts from a few that were especially meaningful to me:

From the first day that I met you, you have been straightforward in your approach to managing the business and people at Seagram. Your no-nonsense style encourages, I believe, employees to concentrate more on positive business results and less on the status quo and office politics . . . I will miss the positive attitude you bring to all business situations and your warm congeniality in social meetings.

—Robert A. Monroe, Seagram

You have been a wonderful role model for many of us at Seagram, representing the epitome of accomplishment. When I think back to 1978, when I joined Seagram, it would have been impossible to comprehend the size and profitability of the business that you and your team have built.

—Michael E. Harbison, Seagram

When I joined Seagram, I specifically asked to meet with you because I liked you and respected your opinions and wanted to hear from you that you believed I had a future here . . . I really looked forward to being a valued player on your team.

—Donard P. Gaynor, Seagram

It has obviously been a significant challenge, but all will agree you have helped transform Seagram into a world power in our industry. Your focus on branded, global, and higher-value products has aided everyone.

—E. Peter Rutledge, Brown-Forman Beverages Worldwide

Hard to believe what the international business was like before you came. I recall one or two of the Italian companies had losses greater than revenues.

—Edward Falkenberg, Seagram

I really admired your tough, clear leadership.

—Bill Logan, Seagram Europe & Africa

This is not a bad time to say how much I have enjoyed our meetings and encounters over the years. And to say, too, how much all of your peers have admired your style at Seagram, and your achievements there, over many years of persistent hard work and energy.

—Michael Jackaman, Allied Domecq, London

I became quite droopy to learn that you, my backbone for ten years, will resign the position of president in June. It is a matter of common knowledge that you made an outstanding contribution to Seagram. I know best that, particularly, you always provided KSL with fair and considerate guidance, and I always appreciated it from the bottom of my heart. I really feel sad to think that I will lose my backbone after June.

—Hironobu Kishindo, Kirin-Seagram Limited, Tokyo

You have always been generous with your time and a friendly word on the way. I want you to know that a lot of the confidence that we have in the relationship with Seagram is built by you personally. We admire the work you have done to make Seagram the global player it is today ... So please, Ed, remember that you have gathered a lot of close friends over the years and we all hope to have the opportunity to enjoy your friendship and company for a long time.

—Curt Nycander, Vin & Spirit, Stockholm

Certainly, Seagram will never be the same without you.

—George F. McCarthy, Allied Domecq, North America

I landed on my feet when I walked away from Seagram. Once I started to see that things were going south with the company, I started laying the groundwork to set up an international liquor distribution company for myself in Asia. It was my backup plan. By the time I left Seagram, my company, Premier Wine and Spirits, was already up and running in the Philippines.

Back then, Seagram operated some of its own distributorships in

Asia. The one in the Philippines was a mess, so I asked Edgar and the Bronfmans if I could take it over, and they said yes. I found a local partner, and together we launched an independent company distributing Seagram brands. When I came in, it was losing money hand over fist, but within a short time, we were making money.

We had a very good team in the Philippines. Naturally, I spent a lot of time there, too. The Filipinos are some of the nicest people I've ever met. I quickly learned that if I treated them well, they would give us a 100 percent effort. I respected that.

After operating in the Philippines for a while, I heard of a business opportunity in the Caribbean. Previously, a monopoly had existed on the liquor industry in the US Virgin Islands, but the US government had stepped in and issued a consent decree that allowed competition to come in. I partnered with my son Paul and another person and created a distributorship there. Thanks to my relationships with people at Seagram, as well as such other brands as Jim Beam, Grey Goose, Campari, Patrón, and Miller beer, among others, we were able to set up a successful business that grew and grew. This was a situation where having good relationships with people throughout the liquor industry really made a difference because I had so many friends at various brands whom I could call on when we were launching this business. There was a lot of price control going on in the Caribbean at the time, so I'd call up my industry friends and say, "Hey, I've heard you're unhappy with your existing situation. I'm coming in and opening up this new company called Premier Wine and Spirits. Would you like to do business with me?" And everybody was happy to jump ship from their existing distributorships and sign on with us.

We distributed beer, wine, and spirits to resorts and hotels in the US Virgin Islands (St. Thomas, St. Croix, and St. John). We also serviced the duty-free market, which was huge in the US Virgin Islands. The downtown areas around the cruise ship ports were full of duty-free liquor stores, and when tourists would disembark from the ships for a day in town, they would stock up on premium brands at great prices. Servicing those cruise ships was an enormous business back then because even the tourists who didn't drink would be so drawn in by the prices that they'd buy liquor as gifts. Every day we'd load up cruise ships with boxes and boxes of liquor purchased by the passengers—quite a lucrative business.

I also bought a company by the name of Antillean Liquors on the island of St. Martin, which supplied the duty-free shops on St. Martin and St. Barts. We held on to that for a while and sold it in 2017.

I had fun owning and running companies in the Philippines and the US Virgin Islands because even though I was ready to walk away from Seagram, I wasn't ready to retire. In my early sixties, I still felt young, and I had too much experience in international business to stop working. Setting up these companies allowed me to keep doing what I did best and to have an opportunity to continue traveling around the world. They also gave me a great opportunity to partner with my children. Ted ran our business in the Philippines, and Paul served as our director of operations in the US Virgin Islands. My daughter, Beth, also worked with us for a year or so in St. Thomas before deciding to pursue other opportunities. I was in charge of these businesses, but because I had wonderful partners and strong teams on the ground, they didn't require me to be on-site running day-to-day operations. I would make five or six trips a year to check in or meet with suppliers, but I never felt I had to micromanage.

Running a business in the US Virgin Islands was challenging because some of the people who my partners and I were dealing with didn't have the same ideas about ethics that we had. But even so, it was a tremendous experience, and I enjoyed the homes I kept in the Philippines and St. Thomas.

We kept our Virgin Islands business going for a while, and then in 2012, we partnered with Glazer's, a distributor based in Dallas, Texas, that had previously focused on national distribution channels in the States. We formed a joint venture, which we named Glazer's Premier Distributors, with Glazer's as the controlling partner. I felt pleased that Premier Wine and Spirits was going to good people at a major company. Paul continued working with Glazer's, which eventually partnered with Southern, another big US distributor. Southern Glazer's bought us out around 2015, although we held on to the warehouses and some other buildings for a couple of years before selling those to Southern Glazer's in 2017.

With the sale of my Caribbean businesses, I retired from the liquor industry. I've kept my hand in it to some extent, making investments here and there and advising various people on a consulting basis. But overall, I'm happy to be out. It's much less of a boom-and-bust market today, and most international markets are fairly well saturated. There are still opportunities, but they're a little harder to find than when I was growing Seagram's global business. These days, my sons are both involved in building liquor brands and funding emerging companies that hope to make it big. Ted's company, Liberty Lighthouse Group, works with brand owners, suppliers, and distributors to create global brand strategies. Ted has brought a lot of unknown brands into the Asian market, and he does very well with it. For his part, Paul works with start-ups, advising them on how to build their brands and succeed in the liquor industry. For many of the newer craft distillers that are too small to be taken seriously by distributors, the goal is either to be purchased by a large company or to increase sales enough to attract the attention of a major distributor. Ted, Paul, and I all enjoy playing a role in assisting small, promising companies to grow into successful players on the global stage, much the way I helped Seagram become a powerhouse back in the '80s and '90s.

It was not easy for me to walk away from Seagram. But doing so opened me up to a range of opportunities that provided fresh prospects and new successes—opportunities I probably would not have had if I had stayed at Seagram. That's the biggest lesson I've learned over the years about knowing when to walk away. Even when you're sad about leaving some amazing experiences behind, you can feel happy looking forward to the new experiences that lie ahead. Change can be difficult, but it usually always makes life more interesting. Isn't that what it's all about?

9

BE A MENTOR

THE VALUE OF HAVING MENTORS IS WIDELY RECOGNIZED IN BUSINESS SCHOOLS TODAY. Most colleges connect business students with successful businesspeople in various ways, including formal mentorship programs and informal networks. I have to admit, I'm a bit envious of this because there was no such thing as mentorship programs when I was growing up. Or if there was, I sure didn't know about them or have access to them. I had learned the value of hard work from my parents and from the people in my community who worked harder in a day than some executives work in a week. But when it came to things like building a corporate career, learning about international opportunities, networking, and figuring out how to succeed in businesses, I was pretty much on my own.

Things turned out fine for me, but I'm sure there are many people from my generation who would have gone much further in their careers if they'd had mentors who could have offered them guidance and advice. And even today, as individuals and business schools recognize the value of mentorships, there's still a shortage of business leaders willing to serve as mentors for the people coming up behind them.

Young people interested in international business—or any type of business or professional career, for that matter—need mentors to advise and support them. And so I challenge you, at every stage of your business career, to make a concerted effort to be a mentor and to give financial support to programs that provide students with professional growth and eye-opening experiences. It takes time, energy, and money, but when you consider the impact it can have on other people, I'm sure you'll agree it's worth everything you put into it.

As I mentioned at the start of the book, I've long supported students at my alma mater, Suffolk University's Sawyer Business School, by funding a program known as the McDonnell Scholars Program. This program provides scholarships for Sawyer's Global Travel Seminars, which arrange overseas experiences for students who might not otherwise be able to afford them. I enjoy knowing that I'm helping students, especially those who, like me, are first-generation college students or the children of immigrants. I like to be able to do something to help these kids, especially when there's no way in hell they'd be able to realize their dream of going overseas to have an international business experience without the money that I donate.

I also love hearing from students who have participated in the program. I've met them at Suffolk events, and some have called or emailed me to ask for career advice. I enjoy learning about their experiences, working at various companies or traveling to different countries. How thrilling for them to be at the start of their careers, looking forward to landing jobs in international business. I'm envious of them sometimes, just starting out on a lifetime of fascinating experiences. I hope they all have as much fun in their careers as I did.

We all have to chip in to help today's students. If you're not donating your time and/or money to your alma mater, I urge you to do so, even if you're just starting out and find yourself with little of either to spare. Even small donations can make a big difference.

How do our donations of money and time help the students of today become successful business leaders of the future? Here's what Suffolk University president Marisa Kelly shared with me about this:

I believe very strongly in the importance of giving back, as Ed has done. Ed had opportunities because of the generosity of others and, especially, because of the GI Bill. If we want people to continue to have opportunities, those of us who have benefitted from help like that have to make it happen. And frankly, for business leaders in general, even if they haven't been beneficiaries of that kind of assistance, they still have a responsibility to students. The future of the economy, the future of the country, and the ongoing productivity and improvement of the world are dependent on next generations being able to move forward and build on the work that their predecessors have done. Without mentoring, without financial support, without internships and other opportunities, it's just not going to happen in the way that we need it to.

The need is especially strong right now. With challenges like the global pandemic and the associated economic crisis, not to mention political divisions, it's easy for anybody—but especially college students—to lose hope and feel like there's no path forward. It's a particularly challenging time for college students to be energized about what's possible. The more that people like Ed and other leaders in the business community can come forward and inspire students with their own stories, their own philanthropy, and their own generosity, the better it will be for students. That kind of role modeling and mentorship create the conditions that will allow this generation to be successful in the way that their predecessors have.

Mentorship isn't just for students, though. Over the course of one's career, it's incredibly important and helpful to have someone who can support you when you have a particular challenge, you're facing a crossroads or a roadblock, or you want to bounce an idea off someone who has more experience than you have. It's so helpful to have someone with the perspective to help you realize that roadblocks can often be opportunities in disguise. We're never too old or too far along in our careers to need that—or to give it.

Being a mentor can be very gratifying. Giving back feels good, whether you're giving time or making a financial donation. There's a real satisfaction in helping people be great at what they do.

We all do better with the support of others. I never forget that I owe much of my success to the GI Bill, which covered my college tuition and made my career possible. It's easy for us to think that our achievements are our own, and although it's true that you can't succeed without hard work, it's also true that nobody makes it on their own. We all stand on the shoulders of the people and institutions that have committed themselves to our success.

THE DIVIDENDS OF MENTORSHIP

In addition to being a boss, I also tried to be a mentor to the people who worked for me. And I try to serve as a role model for friends and family as well. I was never quite sure of the degree to which I had succeeded at any of this until recently, when I asked some friends and family for feedback on how my efforts impacted them. Their comments made me feel very good. I share some of their thoughts not to puff myself up—although they do make me feel happy—but so you can take some lessons from them to apply to your business career and your life.

Steve Herbits, Seagram

The real quality of my relationship with Ed was that any time I got together with him to talk business—whether for lunch or drinks or dinner or a meeting—I never walked away feeling that I wasn't better off for having talked to him. And that didn't happen with many other people—believe me, I'm a very cynical person.

I don't think Ed ever used the words "you should." But he always thought of options that you may not have thought of. And he brought things up in a friendly, easy way. I never witnessed him raising his voice. We spoke as equals, even though I would never say I was an equal with him because his performance at the company was spectacular. He really built the Seagram spirits and wine business.

Many of my conversations with him had to do with strategic issues around the company—not necessarily business strategy but political stuff. We would talk about that in a way that helped me achieve things that I probably wouldn't have been as successful with if I hadn't talked to Ed about them. He made me more successful in my career. There's no question about that.

Vivienne Hylton, Seagram

I met Ed while working as an assistant to Edgar Bronfman Sr. at Seagram. When I first started working for Edgar Sr., I was sort of thrown into the position. I was told to fill in as his assistant for one day, and I was still there eighteen years later. Edgar had an assistant, Maxine, who had been with him for over fifty years, and Edgar put me in the job without my knowing I was to replace Maxine. She made my life hell at first, although we later became very close friends. But at first it was really hard. Ed and Steve Herbits both took me under their wings and helped me through that, mentoring me and making sure I was okay.

I could call on Ed for anything. There were some other assistants who were upset that they didn't get the job as Edgar's assistant, and they made things difficult for me. But Ed was there for me every step of the way. He would tell me, "Don't worry about it. You can do the job. You're going to get through this." Whenever I needed to talk to someone, he was there.

Edgar was a good boss. Really fair. But he could be tough. If he smelled fear on you, then God help you. But I was raised to believe that we're all equal and that you should never have to fear anyone because they have more money than you do. I think Edgar and I got on because I wasn't scared of him.

When Edgar and Ed went to lunch together, we never knew how they would be when they came back. Actually, we did know—they always had a lot of fun at lunch. They were good friends—really good friends. Edgar didn't have many close friends. A lot of people wanted to be his friend because he had money, not necessarily because they liked him. But Ed wasn't like that.

The most important lesson I learned from Ed was to think before you speak and to not let your emotions dictate the way you behave. When I was young, I was a bit hotheaded and would just speak my mind right away. But with Ed's encouragement, I realized that I could phrase things better if I stopped and thought before ranting and raving. That's something Ed really helped me with.

Tony Rodriguez, Seagram

I was in my twenties when I first started working for Ed. One day when I asked him for some advice, he said, "Look, you've got to grab opportunity by the balls. You never know what's going to come along. And if the things that are coming along aren't that exciting, polish that turd and maybe something really good will come out of it."

Ken Herich, Sun Valley

Ed and I met in 1999 in Sun Valley, Idaho. Ed was touring houses, and he saw a house of mine that he liked. He wanted to know who the builder was, and when he was given my name and number, he called me up and invited me to lunch. As we chatted, he said, "I like the work you do, and I like you. Whenever I build a house out here, you'll be the guy to build it." Years went by before he built that house, but true to his word, he asked me to do it. And along the way we built a very good friendship too.

One of the things I've learned from Ed is the awareness of how important it is to work with good people. In contracting, it's easy to get caught up in chasing a juicy deal. But who you're working with is more important than the dollars. The juicy deals aren't worth it if the project is going to be painful or if the guy you'd be working with is a jerk.

I also admire the way Ed rates people on their quality as human beings rather than their status or wealth or what kind of car they drive. Ed's the kind of guy who saves his best tequila for the end of the party, after his guests leave, and shares it with the catering staff. He remembers what it's like to be shanty Irish.

Marty Bart, Seagram

When I was at Seagram in the States and Ed was running the company's international business, Ed told me he thought it would be good for me to see some of the overseas business. He sent me to India, Japan, South America, Europe. This had nothing to do with my everyday work at Seagram in the States, because I was only in charge of sales in the US. I helped him set up distributor organizations around the world, but that's not why he sent me overseas. He just thought it would be good for me to widen my own experiences. I'd never done anything like that before, and it was a tremendous experience for me.

Beth McDonnell

My father loves people. You can be in a restaurant with him, and by the end of the meal, he's made friends with the people at the tables all around you. And the next thing you know, he's invited them all to his house for a party. He has two major parties in Sun Valley every year, and half the people who come are people he's met on chairlifts over the years or at the store that morning. I admire that about him.

Hope Lika

Ed never let failure stop him. If a door got slammed in his face, he just saw it as an opportunity to move forward in a different way—to pick himself up and try it from another angle. He just doesn't have a sense of defeat. Most of us call it quits after frustrations and failures, but he doesn't. I'd like to be more like that.

In addition to mentoring and supporting students, I also enjoy giving back to cultural institutions such as the Sun Valley Music Festival. My interest in supporting the Sun Valley Festival comes from my lifelong love of music. Music and dancing were a big part of my childhood—perhaps because my parents met at a dance. On Sunday afternoons when I was a kid, my family and I would dance to Irish music in our living room. My daughter pokes fun at me because I recently bought a piano for my Sun Valley house even though nobody in our family plays. But I like having it so talented visitors and party guests can entertain me with impromptu performances.

Once when I was a teen, my interest in music led me to an uncomfortable run-in with one of the world's greatest conductors. My father had many jobs over the years, but the one that interested me the most was his position as backstage manager at Symphony Hall on Massachusetts Avenue in Boston. This was in the early 1950s, when I was attending high school nearby at Boston Latin School. My father supervised the cleaning of Symphony Hall and ran the power station in the basement. I used to love listening to the Boston Symphony Orchestra and the Boston Pops, both of which were, at the time, conducted by the brilliant Arthur Fiedler.

Many days after school, I'd walk over to Symphony Hall to meet my father and listen to the orchestra rehearsals. Only orchestra members and Symphony Hall employees were allowed in the building for rehearsals, but I got around that by pretending to sweep the floors in the hall's audience section. My sweeping must not have been very convincing because the musicians would snicker at the kid pretending to work. But nobody said anything to me until one day, when Arthur Fiedler noticed me.

"Kid, come over here," Maestro Fiedler called out from the stage. The musicians were silent as I slowly made my way to him. "Give me that broom," Fiedler demanded. I handed it to him, and then he did something that shocked me and, no doubt, amused the orchestra: he hit me over the head with it. "Get the hell out of here and don't come back," Fiedler yelled.

That was the end of my surreptitious visits to Symphony Hall.

Being able to give to symphony orchestras—and to watch them perform without getting hit on the head—has been one of the great joys of having money. I'm thrilled to be able to support the Sun Valley Music Festival, which is one of the most incredible classical music organizations in the United States. Every summer, top musicians from orchestras around the country participate in the Sun Valley season. Not only do I look forward to attending their performances, but each summer I invite one of the orchestra families to stay at my house during the season. I look forward to it every year and was sorely disappointed when the pandemic prevented me from hosting a symphony orchestra family in 2020. As with so many other situations in which I give my support, I get as much—or perhaps more—from the experience than the recipient.

The joy of giving is that it not only helps someone else, but it makes you feel good also. As the old saying goes, the more you give, the more you receive. That's true of any kind of giving, whether it's mentoring, donating to your alma mater, or supporting cultural institutions. I'm very happy that my success in business has given me the resources to support individuals and organizations that make a difference.

THE NEXT GENERATION

My grandson, Patrick, is one of my favorite people in the world. One of the reasons I wrote this book is because I wanted to compile lessons and stories from my life to pass along to him. Patrick and I have a very special relationship. I've asked him to share a few thoughts about it.

I like spending time with my grandfather. He's a funny guy, and we always have a lot of laughs. We have the same sense of humor. Ever since I was five, he's taken me to Starbucks in the morning when he's in Hilton Head, where I live. He'll show me stuff in the newspaper that he thinks is cool, or we'll talk about sports or stocks or whatever. We also watch TV a lot together. Or sometimes we just drive around. I like to be with him.

His quote is, "Prepare yourself to be lucky." To me, that means working hard and having everything in order, building your own kind of toolbox. When the opportunity arises, you can make the best of it. That's something I try to do. I've been thinking a lot lately about productivity and self-discipline. When I'm thinking productively, I'm keeping up a healthy routine, checking boxes, trying to accomplish goals. Unconsciously I think I'm preparing myself to be lucky every day when I get up and set up my day.

My grandfather works hard. He's done a lot in his life, and now that he's retired, he can just feel good about what he's done. I admire that sense of accomplishment.

He's very observant, and so am I. Sometimes we just people-watch together, and he notices things that surprise me. He listens to me, which I like because listening is important to me, too. I think I'm good at it. And when I ask him questions, he gives me honest, direct answers. I like that.

There have been times when I've fallen behind in school, and he'll give me a call to try to keep me in check. He does it in a way that motivates me and makes me want to work harder. He starts off saying how proud he is of me, and then he reassures me and tells me he loves me for who I am. But then he tells me that I need to get my shit together. Sometimes it's hard for me to ask for help when I need it, but he tells me it's okay to ask for help. I trust his word. I know if he tells me to do something, it's the right thing to do.

He's a good example of why you shouldn't give up. I mean, as corny as that sounds, it's really important. He's achieved so much in his life. Going from what he was born with to where he is now? That's incredible.

10

HAVE FUN ALONG THE WAY

THROUGHOUT THIS BOOK I'VE SHARED LESSONS AND STO-
RIES ABOUT THE MORE SERIOUS SIDE OF BUSINESS: STEPPING
OUT OF YOUR COMFORT ZONE, DOING THE RIGHT THING,
BUILDING STRONG TEAMS, AND SO ON. These practices are critical
for success in today's business world. But as you make your way through
your career, I hope you won't get so tied up in striving for success that
you forget to enjoy yourself. Sure, a business career is full of stressful
situations, difficult challenges, and occasional failures. But it can also be
a hell of a lot of fun. Mine certainly was.

I'd like to wrap this book up by recounting some of my favorite stories
about memorable things that happened during my career. These are some
of the stories I tell when I'm reminiscing with friends and family over a
glass of scotch.

Seagram had a fleet of Gulfstream jets, and I was fortunate enough to
have one available for my use. As a frequent traveler, I appreciated being
able to walk across the street from my Sutton Place apartment on the
East Side of Manhattan to a nearby private helipad, where I would board

a helicopter that would whisk me to Westchester County Airport. The helicopter would land right next to the Gulfstream, and within minutes, I'd be on my way.

What an experience, flying on that Gulfstream. After we took off, a flight attendant would serve whatever meal I had requested. On overnight flights, I'd crawl into a comfortable sofa bed and fall happily asleep, ready to do business the next morning in London or Tokyo or wherever else I was headed. What a pleasure. Flying on that Gulfstream, I never stopped feeling astonished at how lucky I was and how far I had come in life. Edgar Bronfman Sr. always got a kick out of how much I enjoyed flying on the private planes—especially since I was using that equipment to make more money for him. It really was a blast, and it sure beat flying commercial.

I flew so often that I got to know some of the other regulars at the Manhattan helipad I frequented. Most of them were businesspeople like me who traveled regularly. Generally they were nice, friendly people, but one guy stood out as being quite rude and unpleasant. The rest of us would just wait patiently while our helicopter descended from the busy Manhattan sky, even if it was running late, but this infamous New York businessman would stride out to the middle of the helipad and scream up at the pilot, "Get that fucking blade down here now!" The rest of us would just roll our eyes as this guy shouted obscenities into the sky. Fortunately, that's the only time my path ever crossed with Donald Trump.

I took much greater pleasure becoming acquainted with two other presidents: Bill Clinton and Ronald Reagan.

I met President Clinton at the White House in what would turn out to be one of the most exciting moments of my life. My wife, Kay, and I were invited to an event at the White House honoring about ten Irish business-people. Not surprisingly, it took place on St. Patrick's Day. I was in China at the time, and I received the invitation about a week in advance. The day of the event, I flew to Washington, DC, and met Kay there. She had to bring along my tuxedo because I wasn't in the habit of traveling with it. When we were about to leave our hotel for the White House, I realized I hadn't ordered a car, so we were the only guests to arrive by taxi.

What a night it was. When a group of Irish singers began to perform, I just broke down and cried. Not only was I astonished and deeply honored to be at the White House, meeting the president, but I just couldn't help but reflect on what a life I was leading. Here was Ed McDonnell from Hyde Park, the son of a maid and a coal shoveler, standing in the White House shaking hands with the president and first lady of the United States—both of whom couldn't have been nicer to me and my wife. It was the biggest honor of my entire career. How proud my parents would have been, not just because of the accolade I was receiving but because I was being honored as an Irish American. When I told my father years earlier that I had decided to go to college, he asked me why I wanted to be a big shot. I hadn't really known how to answer that question. But on that night, everything felt right. I wish my father could have known that my desire to make something of myself would take me all the way to the White House—not just as Ed McDonnell but as an Irish American and as my father's son.

Meeting Ronald Reagan was also an honor, albeit bittersweet. We met in Scotland about two months after he had finished his second term as president in 1989. Seagram had invited him to give a speech to a group of VIP guests, and everyone was excited to hear what he had to say. For the small group of Seagram executives who had dinner with him beforehand, however, that excitement turned to concern when we discovered that his rumored dementia had progressed further than any of us could have imagined. He struggled to talk with us and seemed confused about where he was. How was he going to deliver a speech, we wondered, when he had trouble holding a dinner conversation? We were quite concerned, but we had no choice but to go ahead with the speech and hope for the best.

What a light-switch moment. He was like a different man when he stood up at the lectern. He started reading his speech and delivered it beautifully. He really was brilliant. If I hadn't seen him at the dinner, I never would have known anything was wrong.

• • •

The team of people with whom I worked at Seagram really enjoyed spending time together. Often after a long day of work, we'd head out for dinner or drinks. In New York, we'd go downstairs to the legendary Four Seasons restaurant, which occupied the ground floor of Seagram headquarters at 375 Park Avenue. My son Paul likes to refer to the Four Seasons as my own private cafeteria because I ate there so often. The fact is, we all did. It was a great place to gather for meetings, for a drink after work, or for dinner with coworkers or clients.

The Four Seasons has an incredible history. Established in 1959, around the time the Seagram Building was built, it had a huge impact on food and restaurant design in New York and the world. Here's how William Grimes described it in the *New York Times* in 2016: "The Four Seasons, probably the most important New York restaurant of the 20th century, Americanized fine dining and set in motion many of the trends that still dominate restaurant culture in the United States. In its time, the Four Seasons was the most modern, the most daring, the most New York restaurant the city had ever seen."

Back when the Four Seasons first opened, the best restaurants served French food; when the Four Seasons created a menu that included regional American dishes made with fresh, local ingredients, it made culinary history. Everyone wanted to dine there, and reservations were difficult to come by—unless you were a Seagram executive, that is.

The Four Seasons was the crown jewel in the Seagram Building, which was commissioned by the Bronfman family and designed by the architects Ludwig Mies van der Rohe and Philip Johnson. The Seagram Building was completed in 1958. Artwork from illustrious American artists was displayed throughout the Four Seasons, which became known as the birthplace of the "power lunch." Some of the celebrities who dined there regularly included Henry Kissinger, Barbara Walters, Anna Wintour, Oscar de la Renta, Martha Stewart, and Jacqueline Kennedy Onassis.

One of my favorite people at the Four Seasons was Alex von Bidder, one of the restaurant's managing partners. I asked Alex, who is still a good friend today, to share some reminiscences from those days.

I started at the Four Seasons in 1976, when I was twenty-six, and I was there for forty-two years. The Four Seasons was in the Seagram Building, and the Seagram executive offices were on the fifth floor. We did a lot of catering upstairs, a lot of wine tastings, a lot of cocktail receptions. They had their own bar up there, their own conference room, but we supplied the labor. I was up there a lot, several times a week.

Downstairs in the restaurant, Edgar Bronfman Sr. always kept the same table. A corner booth. And he always had a bottle of Crown Royal on the table. That was his way of expressing that the Four Seasons was his family's place.

I don't remember meeting Ed—it seems to me that I have always known him. He was always a very friendly, outgoing, happy presence in the restaurant. And of course, he was one of the bosses upstairs. The Seagram people spent a lot of time in the restaurant—they called it their cafeteria.

We always teased Ed that he was drinking cheap wine. Seagram owned some of the best wines in the world, some of the most expensive wines. But he would always drink Sterling wines, which Seagram owned. We'd always say to him, "Ed, why don't you drink something good today?"

From the very beginning, Ed and I had a really good relationship. There was a lot of teasing in both directions. Ed often brought his family to the Four Seasons for Thanksgiving. The McDonnells were one of those families where everybody got along with each other—and you know, that's not normal on Park Avenue in New York, especially during the holidays.

At the Four Seasons, it was my job to remember everything about everybody. Making sure nobody was sitting next to their enemy—that kind of thing. The restaurant was well known for having a pool in the dining room, and the tables that surrounded it were the most popular in the restaurant. Naturally, Ed always assumed that he would have one of those tables, but I couldn't always give it to him. When the restaurant in the Seagram Building closed, we built a new one on Forty-Ninth Street, which was under construction for about two years. Ed would call me whenever he was in town and ask, "Are you open yet? When the hell are you opening? Where am I going to eat?" He always told me he wanted to make sure he wouldn't lose his seat by the pool, even though the new restaurant didn't have a pool. It was always a very joyous relationship.

What Ed represented for me was that even when you are running a multibillion-dollar company, you get a lot more performance out of people by being nice to them. And that's particularly true in restaurants. You know, I saw how my customers treated my staff, and some of them weren't very nice. But Ed was. It's not that he was a softy, but he was proper, and he treated people with respect, friendliness, and patience. If he didn't get what he wanted, he made sure he got it not by yelling or being rude but by using a tone of voice, an expression, that meant seriousness. That's how he got his point across.

There were a lot of domineering guys who were CEOs at the time, especially in the 1980s. For them, it was "my way or the highway." There was no friendliness from them; it was a totally different management style than it is now. But that wasn't the case with Ed. To me, it's always indicative of somebody's character if they're nice to the so-called little people. But to Ed they weren't little people. They were just people.

The Four Seasons moved out of the Seagram Building and to a different New York City location in 2016 and, unfortunately, closed for good in 2019.

• • •

I met many interesting people over the years, but one of my favorites was Princess Margaret, sister of Queen Elizabeth. Seagram sponsored the Grand National, one of the biggest, most prestigious horse races in England. We provided funding to revive it in the 1980s and early 1990s and sponsored various extravagant events connected to the Grand National as well. One year, a horse by the name of Seagram took top honors in the race.

Princess Margaret would attend the Grand National as a representative of the Royal Family. I'll always remember the first time I met her. We were serving as the two hosts for the race that day. I had never met a princess before, and I have to admit, I was pretty nervous about it. I introduced myself and found her to be a woman of few words. I asked her a couple of questions in hopes of getting a pleasant conversation going, but she limited herself to "yes" and "no" answers—which of course made me more nervous. But I wasn't about to give up. I hoped she'd warm up to my next question: "Do you have a home in London?" I asked.

She started to crack up. "Well, I don't, but my mother does," she said. As it turned out, she thought my question was one of the funniest damn things she had ever heard. Not only did it break the ice between us and set the stage for a warm friendship during the following years, but it gave her a story to tell—and from what I heard from others who met her, Princess Margaret told the tale about "that funny American" Ed McDonnell many times.

I met various celebrities during my time at Seagram, but one of my favorite memories is meeting Liza Minnelli. When I was running Seagram, I had joined various exclusive clubs in London. One evening, I was attending a dinner party with my son Paul in one of those clubs. Paul, who was a teenager at the time, excitedly whispered that he had spotted Liza Minnelli across the room. "Oh, she's a good friend of mine," I told him—which was a complete lie, but I thought it would be fun to pretend I knew her. "Would you like to meet her?" I asked.

"Absolutely!" he said.

So I went over to her table, introduced myself, explained what was going on, and asked her if she wanted to play along. Fortunately, she did. A minute later, she came over to Paul with that huge Liza Minnelli smile. "I understand you're Ed McDonnell's son!" she said. Paul was absolutely starstruck. What a peach she was for doing that.

To thank Liza, I offered her box seats for the Wimbledon tennis tournament, which she readily accepted. Unfortunately, however, it rained on the day she was to attend, so we didn't meet up again. But I'll always remember how her eyes lit up when I asked her to pull a fast one on Paul.

FRIENDS WHO ARE LIKE FAMILY

Throughout my life, I've been blessed with wonderful friends. One of the best is Bill Bowen, who agreed to share some memories of our adventures together.

My wife, Caroline, and I met Ed and Kay in the mid-1980s. We live in Hilton Head, and Ed was our almost-next-door neighbor. We spent time with Ed and Kay in New York, Hilton Head, England, and France through the years and have gone on river cruises in Europe with Ed and Hope. Ed and I skied together for years in Europe, Colorado, and Sun Valley. Skiing with Ed was like following a whirlwind—he had incredible power and just wouldn't stop.

Ed is an incredibly generous person. After he retired, he and Kay didn't spend much time in their New York apartment during the winter, so they would give it to us to use as we wished. Once when Ed showed up in the building, the doorman asked him, "Do the Bowens know you're coming?"

On one of our first cruises together, there was an option called the "sterling package." For $200, it covered the cost of your bar bill for the entire cruise. The first night on the boat, the bartender asked us if we'd signed up for the sterling package, and we said no. "Well, I'm signing you up retroactively, because you've already spent more than that in one night." We had a lot of fun together.

When Ed was at Seagram, he often invited me to liquor distributor meetings around the country. People would ask me, "Which distributorship do you own?" And I would say, "I don't have a distributorship. I'm here representing the consumer." Ed was always generous with the perks that came his way—things like center-court seats at Wimbledon or going by private jet to wineries and chateaus in France. What a wonderful time we had together.

I consider Ed one of my best friends. He's a generous, faithful friend. He's always baiting me about politics, but I don't take him seriously. We're on opposite sides politically, but it's never been anything other than a source of amusement for us in our exchanges. He likes to be on the other side of any discussion just to see what havoc he can create. That's the kind of thing Ed loves to do.

When I look back at all of the fun I had and the places I traveled and the interesting people I met during my career, I can hardly believe the way things turned out. My motto from an early age was "Prepare yourself to be lucky." And what luck I had! Lucky to be born into the hardworking McDonnell family. To have access to the GI Bill. To attend and graduate from Suffolk University. To marry my wife, Kay, and to have three fantastic children. To discover a love for international living in London. To be sent to Brazil to run Kibon. To work for a series of terrific companies—especially Seagram. To run my own successful businesses while working alongside my friends and my children. To make so many wonderful friends. And to have the resources to be able to help hundreds of college students have career-changing international experiences. It doesn't get much better than that.

If someone had asked me, as a teenager, what I wanted from life, I'm not sure I would have been able to put my dream into words. But I would have had a rough idea of what kind of experiences I was looking for: Excitement. Success. A world that was completely different than the one in which I had grown up. As it turns out, my life was far more exciting, successful, and different than anything I could have imagined as a kid in Hyde Park.

And now, as I look back on eighty-six years of life, I see that I truly am one of the luckiest people in the world.

REFERENCES

Bronfman, Charles. *Distilled: A Memoir of Family, Seagram, Baseball, and Philanthropy*. HarperCollins Publishers, 2016.

Bronfman, Edgar M. *Good Spirits: The Making of a Businessman*. G. P. Putnam's Sons, 1998.

Cohen, Roberta. "How Pillsbury Is Taking a Giant Step Back into Britain." *Marketing Week*, August 22, 1980.

Cullen, Lisa Takeuchi. "A Fallen Mogul Stirs." *Time*, May 27, 2003.

Faith, Nicholas. *The Bronfmans: The Rise and Fall of the House of Seagram*. St. Martin's Press, 2006.

Grimes, William. "Four Seasons, Lunch Spot for Manhattan's Prime Movers, Moves On." *New York Times*, July 8, 2016.

Hall, Ben. "Business School Celebrates the Legacy of an Alumnus' Travel Scholarship Fund." Suffolk University News, November 5, 2019.

Hollie, Pamela G. "Seagram Revamping in the U.S." *New York Times*, January 17, 1985.

Kandell, Jonathan. "Edgar M. Bronfman, Who Built a Bigger, More Elegant Seagram, Dies at 84." *New York Times*, December 22, 2013.

Killoran, Ellen. "Rejected Time Inc. Bidder Edgar Bronfman Brought Down His Family's Business." *Fortune*, November 29, 2016.

Leinster, Colin. "The Second Son Is Heir at Seagram." *Fortune*, March 17, 1986.

Milner, Brian. "The Unmaking of a Dynasty." *Cigar Aficionado*, March/April 2003.

Saltmarsh, Matthew, and Eric Pfanner. "French Court Convicts Executives in Vivendi Case." *New York Times*, January 21, 2011.

Shapiro, Arthur. *Inside the Bottle: People, Brands, and Stories.* A/M Shapiro & Associates, 2016.

Sloane, Leonard. "International Post Filled at Seagram." *New York Times*, June 9, 1981.

Sorkin, Andrew Ross. "The Refrain That Follows Bronfman." *New York Times*, March 4, 2008.

ABOUT THE AUTHOR

Ed McDonnell served as president and CEO of the Spirits and Wine Group at The Seagram Company, one of the most successful beverage alcohol brands in the world. He grew the Spirits and Wine Group from a largely North American-based operation to a $5 billion global business. On his watch, Seagram became the world's largest producer and distributor of distilled beverages.

McDonnell also held executive positions at Pillsbury and General Foods, where he oversaw operations in Latin America, Europe, and Asia. After leaving Seagram, he ran several of his own successful liquor distribution companies in Asia and the Caribbean.

The son of Irish immigrants, McDonnell grew up in South Boston and is a proud graduate of Suffolk University's Sawyer Business School. He funds Suffolk's popular McDonnell Scholars Program, which over the past twenty-five years has supported more than three hundred business students participating in intensive international travel seminars in countries around the world.

Now retired, McDonnell has homes in New York City; Hilton Head, South Carolina; and Sun Valley, Idaho.